ENDORSEMENTS

"Well, I found my new devotional guide! I've known for some time that Schleiermacher's thought was fruitful. But Chad Bahl brings the ideas to our daily lives. This book sparks new ideas about how I can incorporate the insights of the Father of Modern Theology or criticize what I don't like. I'm putting this next to my bed for evening reading!"

— **Thomas Jay Oord**, author of *Open and Relational Theology*

"Today, Friedrich Schleiermacher is most often read academically, but *Mornings with Schleiermacher* is a book that gets to the heart of his spiritual contributions by approaching the Father of Modern Theology as if he were a spiritual guide and not merely one of the most significant theologians to have ever lived. This framing gives the Monologen—Schleiermacher's spiritual autobiography—its proper space to be more than just an academic text but also a potential source of spiritual inspiration and growth. In that regard, this project is a novel and refreshing look at Schleiermacher, one to spark interest in his theology but, most of all, to foster the kind of spiritual renewal Schleiermacher hoped for his readers. It is spiritually and intellectually stimulating thanks to a helpful introduction and the 30-day musings by Chad Bahl, which pairs nicely with the Monologen."

— **Stephen D. Morrison**, author of *Schleiermacher in Plain English*

"Solid theological reflection involves the interplay of vision, promise, and practice, or head, heart, and hands. Chad Bahl's *Mornings with Schleiermacher* fulfills this promise. Bahl presents Schleiermacher's theological vision clearly and insightfully; he enables the reader to experience first-hand Schleiermacher's religion of absolute dependence on a graceful God; and he presents daily meditations that make Schleiermacher come alive in the reader's experience. This text invites you to get to know the father of modern liberal theology, see the world with his eyes, and experience God in an intimate and transformative way. So, grab a cup of coffee and spend a morning with Schleiermacher, and then be prepared to see your world with new eyes!"

— **Bruce Epperly**, author of *Taking a Walk with Whitehead*

"I'm not big on devotionals, but this one is different! Chad Bahl masterfully introduces readers to his good friend, Schleiermacher, encouraging deep and engaging conversation. These reflections followed by meaningful writing prompts, serve as a beautiful introduction into the mind of the Father of Liberal Theology. Grab a cup of coffee, or a cold beer, and allow Chad to guide you into the depths and treasures of this great theologian. All that to say... I guess I like devotionals again!"

— **Josh Patterson**, Host of the (Re)thinking Faith Podcast

"For those wanting to dip their toes into the work of Friedrich Schleiermacher or who have been overwhelmed by academic texts in the past, this work offers an enjoyable and easily digestible understanding of Schleiermacher's theology, one that we can all benefit from!"

— **Elizabeth Enns Petters**, co-host of the Deconstructing Mamas podcast

Daily Readings by
CHAD BAHL
Musings and The Monologen

A Devotional Inspired by the Father of Modern Theology
MORNINGS
with
SCHLEIERMACHER

The chapter, "Schleiermacher's Soliloquies," is a reproduction of Friedrich Schleiermacher's *The Monologen,* and has been reformatted from its original form in public domain by Rob Edwards. A great deal of work went into the project, and we owe him a great debt of gratitude for the fine work he did.

Cover design and interior layout by Matthew J. Distefano
Cover image by Keith Giles

ISBN 978-1-964252-12-4
Printed in the United States of America

Published by Quoir
Chico, California
www.quoir.com

CONTENTS

It is rarely easy to narrow down a dedication to one person, but this one wasn't very difficult. *Mornings with Schleiermacher* and the success of my other writings, including *Deconstructing Hell*, would not have been possible without the kind, wise, and generous guidance of my teacher and advisor at Northwind Theological Seminary, Thomas Jay Oord.

Thank you for the time you take with me, as with all of your students, investing yourself in each of our interests, making them better, and helping to give them purpose.

TIMELINE OF SIGNIFICANT DATES

Adapted from Friedrich Schleiermacher, *Hermeneutics and Criticism and Other Writings*, Andrew Bowie, ed. (Cambridge: Cambridge University Press, 1995), xxxii-xxxiii.

1768: Schleiermacher born in Breslau, Germany, on November 21st

1783–5: Schleiermacher attends Moravian boarding school

1787–90: Schleiermacher attends the University of Halle

1790–3: Schleiermacher works as a house tutor in Schlobitten in East Prussia

1793–6: Schleiermacher serves as pastor in Landsburg, Germany

1796–1802: Schleiermacher among Romantic circle in Berlin, including Fridrich Schlegel

1797: Schleiermacher becomes reformed chaplain at the Charite hospital in Berlin

1799: Schleiermacher publishes *On Religion: Speeches to its Cultured Despisers*

1800: Schleiermacher publishes *The Monologen*

1803–6: Schleiermacher assumes the post of university preacher at Halle

1804–28: Schleiermacher publishes a German translation of Plato

1809: Founding of the University of Berlin with Schleiermacher as secretary to the founding commission

1809–34: Schleiermacher at the University of Berlin as professor of theology

1810–34: Schleiermacher as preacher at the Holy Trinity Church in Berlin

1821: Schleiermacher publishes *The Christian Faith*

1834: Death of Schleiermacher on February 6th

"No choicer gift can a man give another than his spirit's intimate converse with itself. For this affords the highest boon there is, a clear and undistorted insight into a free being. No gift is more enduring, for nothing can destroy the satisfaction which such an insight has once granted you, and its intrinsic truth assures your love so that you will delight in beholding it again. None is surer proof against the lust and guile of others, since it arouses no desire that is not spiritual, and offers no secondary attractions that could lead to its abuse. If anyone stands aloof, and looks askance at this precious treasure, attributing to it absurd features which your honest eye does not detect, let no such idle mockery rob you of your joy. Heed it as little as I shall let myself repent of having shared with you that which I had to give. Come, take the gift, ye who can understand my spirit's thought! May my feeling here intoned be an accompaniment to the melody within yourselves, and may the shock which passes through you at the contact with my spirit, become a quickening impulse to your life."

— **Friedrich Schleiermacher**
Offering[1] from *The Monologen*

PREFACE

MAKING THE MOST OF MORNINGS WITH SCHLEIERMACHER

"If anyone still speaks today in Protestant theology as though he were still among us, it is Schleiermacher. We *study* Paul and the reformers, but we *see* through the eyes of Schleiermacher and think along the same lines he did."

— **Karl Barth,** *The Theology of Schleiermacher*[1]

HOW TO READ THIS BOOK

MORNINGS WITH SCHLEIERMACHER IS written as an introduction to the life and thoughts of the man who became known as the Father of Modern Theology. It is intended as a volume you can explore, enjoy, and interact with as you familiarize yourself with Friedrich Schleiermacher's big ideas. At its core, this book is a devotional for personal reflection. But it is also a work that provides multiple pathways toward spiritual growth through daily readings, biography, and the reproduction of a classic monograph.

Mornings begins as a 30-day experience of reflections. Each day, you will start with a brief passage from the writings of Schleiermacher, followed by some thoughts and questions to consider. Each devotion is designed to take 10-15 minutes to complete, though you may choose to use them as a catapult for deeper consideration.

After the devotional content, you will encounter my critical introduction to the life and major themes of Friedrich Schleiermacher's work, entitled *Father of Modern Theology: An Introduction to the Monologen*. It is notable that this section is technically written and intended as a more thorough companion to the brief introduction offered in this preface. Give it a try, but do not be frustrated if you find the content a bit too academic. If you do, go ahead and skip to the end of the section. There you will find a helpful chapter-by-chapter summary of Schleiermacher's *The Monologen* to help prepare you for the masterpiece itself!

The final portion of this volume is a reproduction of *The Monologen*. Considered Schleiermacher's 'spiritual autobiography,' he utilizes the rhetoric of monologue to paint an intimate depiction of his inmost spiritual thoughts. *The Monologen* consists of five soliloquies (titled *Reflection*, *Soundings*, *The World*, *Prospect*, and *Youth and Age*). Each of these provides a unique perspective on the life lived through the lens of the 'inner self.'

A Progressive's Devotional

This book is written to be a progressive devotional, but it is also appropriate for anyone who desires to reflect on their spiritual journey, regardless of where they fall on the dogmatic spectrum. Schleiermacher has occasionally been called the Father of Liberal Theology. This is largely because of his ecumenical stance toward many doctrinal issues. He helped recenter faith in a way that prioritized the experience of a relationship with God and spoke out strongly against the extremes of both biblical literalism and spiritual relativism. His grounding principle was the redemptive work of Christ. As such, he had little time for disputes, which would only serve to segregate the Church along partisan lines. This devotional is written in that same spirit.

SCHLEIERMACHER'S MAJOR THEMES

When it comes to the practice of the Christian faith, for many reading this text, Friedrich Schleiermacher is the most consequential name you have never heard. As Karl Barth's above quote implies, today's believer views their faith through the lens Schleiermacher bequeathed. But oddly, more conservative branches of Christianity have largely silenced such attribution.[2] Because of this, it is worth mentioning what made his 'big ideas' so meaningful (and, for many, controversial) before proceeding to the devotional content.

Faith through Feeling

Born in 1768, Friedrich Schleiermacher was a child of the Great Enlightenment Period. During this time, humanity's capacity for discerning truth through reason alone dominated over any alternative pathway. Because of this, matters of faith were deconstructed. They were seen as anti-intellectual, unsophisticated, and mystical. Schleiermacher spoke out against this prevailing perspective. He admonished these 'cultured despisers' of religion, insisting that viewing faith through the prevue of reason was missing the point altogether. In his famous apologetic work, *On Religion*, Schleiermacher responded to those for whom faith could be reduced to its rationalized parts, admonishing, "If you have only given attention to these dogmas and opinions, therefore, you do not yet know religion itself, and what you despise is not it."[3] For Schleiermacher, religion's essence was founded not in reason but in the *experience* of God. More specifically for him, faith was grounded in *feeling*.

Although this reframing gave religion a reliable apologetic, many orthodox thinkers bristled at this suggestion. Schleiermacher sparked almost immediate criticism that he was turning spirituality into a subjective practice. Indeed, this was a claim to which Schleiermacher was forced to respond throughout his career. But he denied that what he meant by feeling (*Gefühl* in German) was a subjective happening. Instead, he argued it was a deep-founded *in-*

tuition located in what he called the 'immediate self-consciousness'[4] of all people. For Schleiermacher, Enlightenment thinking could not reason away God because *reason* was not the grounding principle of faith. Religion, at its core, was a feeling.

Feeling of Absolute Dependence

Perhaps Schleiermacher's most well-known claim was that the essence of religion is the "feeling of being absolutely dependent in relation with God."[5] For him, no greater summation represented the meaning of faith. Once humanity recognized its essential need for God, the 'feeling of dependence' would bestow a freedom for it to live to its highest potential. Humanity can interact with the world around it. But it can never realize the complete satisfaction of any desire outside of the creating and sustaining power of the Divine.

God-Consciousness

In contrast to that which robs us of the experience of God, Schleiermacher felt it only necessary to pursue avenues of religious truth that contributed to developing one's 'God-consciousness.'[6] If a dogma or tradition of the Church did not contribute to this ultimate ideal, he did not deem it an essential part of faith. Schleiermacher's principle of God-consciousness allowed him a basis for prioritizing doctrinal pursuits. For him, matters of Church community and Divine activity trumped the divisive landmines of biblical authority and ceremonial practice.

In short, it can accurately be said that, for Schleiermacher, the cultivation of *God-consciousness* leads to a *feeling of absolute dependence* on the Divine, which allows us to *experience* religion in a way that Enlightenment thinkers had neglected to consider.

Polymath

While Schleiermacher's recognition as the Father of Modern Theology gives him a place of prominence in the history of Christianity, it is far from his only contribution to it. Schleiermacher was a true polymath with wide-ranging accomplishments of vital importance for today's faith. Schleiermacher was considered the *Father of Hermeneutics* for the system of biblical interpretation he created. Schleiermacher moved the focus of biblical authorship away from the mystical realm of the Divine and toward the writers themselves. He believed that the meaning of a text must include considerations such as historical context, author intent, use of language, and literary technique. He deemed it not only possible but necessary "to understand the text just as well, and then better than the author himself understood it."[7] Schleiermacher's methods introduced a new way of studying the Bible that had been largely unexplored but is today considered of foundational importance.

Schleiermacher also contributed to the ongoing dialogue within Christian ethics. In his writings, he emphasized the implications for ethical practice, not just for the individual, but for the Church community. He stated, "Nobody in the Christian Church can claim something as true for himself without at the same time claiming it is valid for the church" as a whole.[8] And he focused on the implications of actions on the larger community, withdrawing ethics from the realm of the individual altogether. Schleiermacher additionally emphasized the study of ethics as a contextual practice. For him, "we cannot be certain whether everything that we now establish as right and good will be so regarded in the future any more than we now accept everything that had validity in other times."[9]

Schleiermacher was an accomplished academic, helping found the University of Berlin and serving tenures both there and the University of Halle. He was a pastor, preaching at the renowned Holy Trinity Church in Berlin for 24 years, rarely missing a Sunday. Schleiermacher also translated the majority of Plato's works into his native German tongue and wrote several historical-critical works that were well ahead of their time.[10] The collected writings of Schleiermacher consist of over forty volumes. He is indeed a man worthy of our unmitigated time and attention.

MY HOPE IN WRITING

My hope in writing this current volume is two-fold. First, in studying the devotional content and reading what follows, I hope you will be inspired to learn more about the life and teachings of Friedrich Schleiermacher. He has been as or more impactful in my spiritual journey than any other theologian. If this book accomplishes little else than raising awareness of his contributions to the Christian faith, the effort will be worthwhile. Secondly (and more importantly), I hope what follows inspires you along your spiritual journey. Wherever you may find yourself, may this book meet you and guide you further along. May you find hope in its pages and a sense of wonder as you consider life's deep, spiritual questions. May the *Mornings* you spend lead to days of joy, of hope, and of peace.

— **Chad**

DAY 1

LED BY LOVE

"Love is a disposition, and a disposition can
never be commanded."

— Friedrich Schleiermacher
Introduction to Christian Ethics

WE ARE INHERENTLY RULE followers. We want to know that we are doing the right thing. Tell us how to act and what box to check, and we can be confident we are heading down the correct path.

For some, however, seeking a list of 'to-dos' can be a stressful proposition. Uncertainty is never as anxiety-inducing as when intuition is stripped from the equation. What's more, is an act ever moral if it is performed purely from a place of obligation?

Schleiermacher addresses this issue in the above quote. Jesus states that believers will be known by their love (John 13:35). But no act is ever inherently loving. Nor is morality reducible to mere gestures. Love is the disposition from which moral action occurs.

When we live from a place of love, we will act morally. When love is absent, so is virtue.

When we realize this truth, we are free from the constraints of living by a set of rules. We can allow our lives to be led, not by lists, but by love.

MUSINGS

"No act is inherently loving." Do you agree with this statement? Why or why not?

Is it possible for two people to do the same thing, and only one of them to be acing morally? In what way?

Can a life lived from love ever be free from rules? How so?

DAY 2

ORIGINAL PERFECTION

"The predisposition to God-consciousness,
as an inner impulse...form[s] man's original perfection."

— **Friedrich Schleiermacher**
The Christian Faith

CONSERVATIVE CHRISTIANS HAVE MADE careers off of telling us that we are inherently sinful, evil, and debased people. To grow up inside the evangelical church today means being taught you are worthless outside of a certain set of salvific beliefs. This is unfortunate and unnecessarily demeaning towards a creation fashioned by God, in the image of God.

In his great dogmatic work, *The Christian Faith*, Schleiermacher instead directs attention to what he calls our 'original perfection.' By this, he means our inherent capability to intuit and commune with God.

For him, "The totality of finite existence...works together in such a way as to make possible the continuity of the religious self-consciousness." In other words, everything that exists, including us in our deepest instincts, perceives and points to the One who is Creator and Sustainer of all.

4

It is such a freeing feeling to know that you are good enough AS YOU ARE. You are beautiful, loved and able to enjoy the fruits of the humanity you were made to partake in.

You are not originally sinful. Because of God, you have the great gift of original perfection.

MUSINGS

What baggage comes from being told you are a sinful person?

How might your view of yourself change if you realized you were created to commune with God...as you are?

How might your view of others be different in light of 'original perfection'?

DAY 3

Open-Mindedness

"The figurative sayings of Christ, which have led to a state of
irremediable misery for those who die outside of fellowship
with Christ being accepted as the counterpart of eternal bliss,
will, if more closely scrutinized, be found insufficient to support any such conclusion."

— Friedrich Schleiermacher
The Christian Faith

I USED TO BELIEVE in hell. I don't anymore. At least not in the sense that it
is a place of eternal conscious torment for those who refuse to repent their
sins.

But I certainly grew up believing it to be true. It was a central tenet of my
evangelical faith. Sure, God was loving. But God was also just, and sin could
not go unpunished. As such, my mission was to save as many as I could from
this unspeakable demise.

I traveled the world with the motivation of creating converts. If I could
get just one person to check the box and recite the prayer of salvation, my

mission would be successful. My job was done, and one more soul would be won before the world burned.

It took me decades to realize that I was the one missing the mark. I was so concerned about the recitation of a prayer, that I was doing very little to demonstrate God's heart...to serve, to listen, and to love. I was propagating fear, not cultivating communion. What's more, I failed to be open to learning what it was God wanted to teach me through others. (Why would I need to do that when I held all the answers?)

What was instrumental in changing my belief in hell as eternal conscious torment was the realization that the Bible doesn't teach it. I had been so close-minded that I wasn't willing to objectively study the Scriptures in a way that allowed me to see things differently.

Once I deconstructed hell, I didn't lose faith, I found freedom in it. I am still passionate about my beliefs. I am still in love with God, enthralled by the Gospel, and I still desire to spend my days living out the faith I confess. But I am a better Christian. I see others not just for how I can change them, but for how I can love them, and receive love from them. I speak with others, not just for what I can persuade them of, but for what I can learn.

I am more open-minded. I am convinced now more than ever that I must never feel so confident in my beliefs as not to be willing to change my thinking when presented with compelling evidence.

Beliefs and dogmas are a tool to serve faith. They should never be its object.

MUSINGS

Does today's reading resonate with you? If so, how?

Describe a time when you reconsidered a belief central to your faith.

What steps can you take to be open-minded towards those who believe differently than you?

DAY 4

SCHLEIERMACHER'S DECONSTRUCTION

"Whenever people among us have lost
interest in knowing of God,
it has always been due to the prevailing exposition
rather than to the idea itself."

— Friedrich Schleiermacher
On the Glaubenslehre

FRIEDRICH SCHLEIERMACHER WAS RAISED the son of a Reformed minister. He was sent to attend school in a Moravian community at an early age, where he gained a passion for the experience of the Christian faith. The Moravians were known for their commitment to uninterrupted prayer (which lasted over one hundred years!), and to the work of missions. They even sold themselves into slavery to get the chance to reach unevangelized regions.

But for all he grew to appreciate about the piety of the Moravians, Schleiermacher craved forbidden knowledge. He would sneak banned books into the strict community. On one occasion, he was nearly expelled after being caught reading Kant's *Critique of Practical Reason*.

Schleiermacher would eventually seek permission to leave the community and pursue higher education at a secular institution, no longer being able to affirm doctrines core to the Moravian faith, such as the divinity of Christ and the need for a blood atonement.

When his studies were complete at the University of Halle, Schleiermacher felt torn. He was torn about his faith and torn about his future. He still felt drawn to ministry but was unsure how effective he could be. He was often depressed and even contemplated suicide.

It would turn out that accepting a position to be a tutor at a local Count's estate would prove lifesaving for him. He would say of that period, "Here my sense for the beauty of human fellowship first awakened." He would even fall in love for the first time on this estate.

Schleiermacher began to recall the pious experiences he once had as a Moravian, but he would look at them through a new set of lenses, through all that he learned at Halle and through the beauty of companionship with his fellow man. He would still call himself a Moravian, but now "a Moravian of a Higher Order."

With a passion for God and community reignited, Schleiermacher would go on to achieve heights he would never have imagined. Through his numerous writings, preaching, and scholarship, he would focus less on the dogmas of faith and more on the experience of it. This reframing would become so impactful that he would go on to become known as the Father of Modern Theology.

If you find yourself questioning or deconstructing your faith, you are in good company. Sometimes we must lose what is most important to us in order to find ourselves anew.

MUSINGS

Name a time when you felt compelled to deconstruct a previously held belief.

In what ways does it help knowing that others have and are going through their own deconstruction process?

If you currently find yourself deconstructing, what step can you take today to find peace in the midst of loss? If you are not deconstructing, how can you help someone who is?

DAY 5

THE GIFT

"Come, take the gift, ye who can understand my spirit's thought! May my feelings here intoned be an accompaniment to the melody within yourselves, and may the shock which passes through you at the contact with my spirit, become a quickening impulse in your life."

— Friedrich Schleiermacher
The Monologen

IN 1799, SCHLEIERMACHER PUBLISHED his first work, *On Religion: Speeches to its Cultured Despisers*. This was done only after much prodding by a close friend to put the words of his heart from pen to paper.

Though today considered the Father of Modern Theology, Schleiermacher never considered himself a skilled author. But he possessed two qualities in spades: a passion for knowledge and a love of humanity.

These attributes would shine through in his debut writing and quickly resulted in the publication of what would be called his 'spiritual autobiography' the following year: *The Monologen*. Schleiermacher discovered that he had an unrealized gift that must be given to others...himself.

May we be bold enough to grasp this is a gift we all possess. We all have something unique to offer. We all have insight that can benefit others. We all have passions and perspectives that can light a fire in someone's heart.

Let today be the day you decide to share your gift.

MUSINGS

What passion do you possess that you have yet to offer others?

What is stopping you, and what can help you overcome this barrier?

Who in your life can benefit from your gift? What step can you take today to share it?

DAY 6

Reason or Experience?

"To hear them discourse on the world today, one would imagine the thundering voice of their mighty reason had burst the chains of ignorance, that they had at last succeeded in setting up a perfect portrait of human nature, which formerly had been painted obscurely in colors of darkness, so as to be scarcely recognizable."

— Friedrich Schleiermacher
The Monologen

As the Enlightenment came to an end, Schleiermacher penned his *Monologen* in part as a response to what he deemed as the dark side of the Age of Reason.

Many thinkers during this time had reasoned away the need for God, for a dependence on the Divine. Man sat boldly on the throne of the world, Reason his sword, Knowledge his plated armor.

Schleiermacher lamented this sentiment. For he had discovered something beyond Reason's grasp. He called it a 'taste for the Infinite.' This 'taste' was an intuition that something much greater than himself existed. Because he experienced the Divine, he could ground his thinking in the centering principle that God was with him.

May we have this same attitude. May we carry with us this same hope. And may we always care less about the world we try to create through our own reason than we do the experience of the One who has created us.

MUSINGS

How does today's reading resonate with you? Do you tend to rely on Reason or Experience?

What in your life (if anything) has allowed you to experience God?

What step can you take today to trust in God's existence despite any reasoning to the contrary?

DAY 7

COMPLACENCY

"O, how deeply I despise this generation, which plumes itself
more shamelessly than any previous one ever did, which can
scarcely endure the belief in a still better future and reviles
everyone who dedicates themselves thereto."

— Friedrich Schleiermacher
The Monologen

SCHLEIERMACHER PENNED THESE WORDS in 1800, as the Enlightenment
ended, and Romanticism took form. The time of great thinkers such as
Immanuel Kant, David Hume, John Locke, and Frances Bacon, the Enlightenment marked a period of climax in both philosophy and science. What else
was left for humanity to achieve, having unlocked the mysteries of life itself?

Looking back, in the wake of all that was to come, we know there was much
more. And this is the heart behind Schleiermacher's rebuke.

Impulse is never so deceptive as when it spurs one on toward an attitude
of complacency. Humanity is at its best when it admits it is small and the
Universe a vast trove of undiscovered treasure. She is at her worst when she
believes there is nothing more than that which appears plainly before her.

May we never become so prideful in our knowledge to think we have reality firmly in our grasp.

To *know* is folly. To *seek* is the greatest wisdom.

MUSINGS

When was a time you thought you had all the answers, only to discover there was more to know?

How can *certainty* prevent you from discovering yourself more deeply?

How can *certainty* prevent you from knowing God more deeply?

DAY 8

What is Religion?

"If you have only given attention to these dogmas and opinions, therefore, you do not know religion itself, and what you despise it is not."

— Friedrich Schleiermacher
On Religion

For the Father of Modern Theology, we err when we focus first on the opinions, dogmas, and usages of faith. To him, faith that is grounded in anything but our relationship with God is off-center.

Fear...dogmatism...biblical literalism...All of these forces have caused great hurt. They have driven well-intended seekers of truth away from embracing that which is fundamental to humanity's well-being. Schleiermacher proposed that the essence of religion was none of these things. To him, instead, it was the "feeling of absolute dependence on God."

Reflecting on religion, Schleiermacher would say, "It helped me as I began to sift the faith of my fathers and to cleanse thought and feeling from the rubbish of antiquity. When the God and the immortality of my childhood vanished from my doubting eyes it remained with me."

There is an important place in faith for doctrine. But it cannot be the foundation of belief. If it is, we risk losing God when our opinions change. It is the 'feeling of dependence' that we must cultivate first.

Like any relationship, we must pursue the presence of the person before we can establish what is or isn't true about them.

Connect with God today, first and foremost. Let all else come naturally from that sacred place.

MUSINGS

How does Schleiermacher's definition of religion differ from your own?

Describe a time when your opinions of 'doctrines and dogmas' changed?

What step can you take today to deepen your dependence on God?

DAY 9

BEAUTY AND PEACE

"One can say that the distinguishing essence of Christianity
exists not in action, but in rest...The highest human perfection
is portrayed as rest in the contemplation of God
and God's self."

— Friedrich Schleiermacher
Introduction to Christian Ethics

"God does not create the world, he saves it; or, more accurately,
he is the poet of the world, with tender patience leading it by
his vision of...beauty."

— Alfred North Whitehead
Process and Reality

WHAT IS THE HIGHEST ideal in life? For the Father of Modern Theology, it
was the achievement of inner peace, of rest. For many, it is the creation of that
which is beautiful. Others may want to disagree saying, "No, the highest ideal
must be pleasing God, honoring God's will, and obeying God's commands."

This sentiment may be valid. But the question is begged, "What is it that pleases God?"

To answer, we should reference the words of Jesus, when he states, "Peace I leave you" (John 14:27), and Solomon when he declares that God aims to make "everything beautiful in its own time." (Eccles. 3:11). *We are given Peace so that we can join God in the creation of Beauty.*

If your day can begin and end with these two aims, I believe you will be living in the center of God's ideals for you.

Feelings of stress, anxiety, and despair are what happens when the aim of creating Beauty from a place of Peace is neglected. They are the war wounds of those who strive, whose priorities are misaligned, and whose ultimate hopes are misplaced.

Though society may want you to believe the opposite, stress is not the barometer of achievement. In a sense, it is its fiercest competitor.

MUSINGS

Do the ideals of Beauty and Peace resonate with you? Why or why not?

What in your life prevents you from achieving these ideals?

What step can you take today to move towards Beauty and Peace?

DAY 10

AGELESS YOUTH

"Be not a fool to prophecy the spirit's strength in terms of
time, for time can never be its measure...The decline of vigor
and of strength is an ill that man inflicts upon himself; old age
is but an idol prejudice, an ugly fruit of the mad delusion that
the spirit is dependent on the body!"

— **Friedrich Schleiermacher**
The Monologen

IT IS OF NOTE that Schleiermacher penned these words at the age of thirty-two. It would be interesting to know if he would have rephrased his passionate prose as physical age overtook his own body.

Nonetheless, his poignancy remains enshrined in this great work, and it is clear that Schleiermacher lived his life with the fullness of one who believed every word of it.

From an early age, he undertook the translation of both Aristotle and Plato into German, his native tongue...He wrote diversely on topics including philosophy and Christian ethics...He co-founded the University of Berlin...He spent decades as the Lead Pastor of Trinity Church in Berlin...His work in interpretation earned him the title Father of Hermeneutics...His work in dogmatics earned him the title Father of Modern Theology. Of him the adage was certainly true: Age is but a state of mind.

All bodies grow old, but not all spirits do. Live with passion. Live with vigor. Live a life of love, embracing each moment as if it were your last. May your affections be the kindling that ignites your heart's desires. May your youth be ageless.

MUSINGS

How can physical age impact our passions and desires?

How can you reframe your thinking in a way which breaks the bonds and limitations which age arbitrarily assigns?

What step can you take today to live a life of Ageless Youth?

DAY 11

MISUNDERSTOOD

"The best that can be said of me is I am
not what they take me to be."

— **Friedrich Schleiermacher**
The Christian Faith

AFTER THE RELEASE OF the first edition of *The Christian Faith*, Schleiermacher received a barrage of reproofs from the critics and thought leaders of the day. Charges against him ranged from that of pantheism (the belief that God and creation are one and the same) to Hegel's famous accusation that Schleiermacher's philosophy equated the mentality of humans to that of dogs. After all, what is the difference between humans and animals if both are driven solely by instinct and emotion? (This was a common representation made by Schleiermacher's critics because of his emphasis on the experience of faith.)

Of course, a cursory reading of Schleiermacher's great dogmatic work would prove his critics misguided. But that's the point, isn't it?

How often in our lives do we treat people by their caricature and not their character? It is much easier to grasp onto a single idea or antidote and view someone through the monolithic lens of a broad brush.

Let us resist this base tendency with ferocity. May we always reserve judgment, even as we take the time to understand.

MUSINGS

Describe a time when someone's misunderstanding of you caused you to be hurt.

Describe an instance when you did not take the time to understand someone else.

What step can you take today to understand someone better, whose perspective is different than your own?

DAY 12

Despise Not Religion

"How unjustly, therefore, do you reproach religion with loving persecution, with being malignant...with making blood
flow like water...Blame those who corrupt religion, who flood
it with an army of formulas and definitions, and seek to cast it
into the fetters of a so-called system."

— **Friedrich Schleiermacher**
On Religion

For Schleiermacher, religion in its most basic form was a 'sense and taste for the Infinite.' It was the intuition that God existed. And, if God existed, the dependence we should place on such an infinite Being naturally followed.

For him, religion was not the doctrines or dogmas that spur debates and controversies. It was not the prejudices and preconceived notions that are used to justify endless war. And it was certainly not the judgments and condemnations that lead to generational fear and hurt.

Religion was the experience of an intimate relationship with the Divine. For the Father of Modern Theology, this was religion, the birthing hour of all good things.

May we begin to perceive religion without the 'army of formulas and definitions' with which we often cloud it.

If we can somehow take this simple, first step, we will find the Universe standing in wait.

MUSINGS

What emotion does the word 'religion' evoke in you?

How does Schleiermacher's reframing of the word resonate with you?

What step can you take today to deepen your relationship with God?

DAY 13

GOD-CONSCIOUSNESS

"Hence [it] must not be understood that the orthodox doctrine of the Trinity is to be regarded as an immediate or even
necessary combination of utterances concerning the Christian
self-consciousness."

— Friedrich Schleiermacher
The Christian Faith

FOR SCHLEIERMACHER, THE ESSENCE of faith was grounded in what he
called 'God-consciousness.' By this he meant our experience of God, or our
awareness of God.

In his eight-hundred-page dogmatic tome, he was quick to point out
which doctrines were central to the Christian faith, and which were not. His
key criteria: Does it draw the believer to a deeper relationship with God? Does
it develop her God-consciousness?

Doctrines such as the Trinity, the virgin birth, the existence of angels, etc.,
may be important to consider but can never be seen as essential to understand
in order to partake in the Christian faith. For Schleiermacher, there was a
great divide between knowledge about God and the experience of God.

When academic acumen becomes a litmus test for true belief, faith has lost its way.

Schleiermacher envisioned a united Church that sought to heal division, not create it through petty disputes and controversies.

Let us never hold onto our doctrine with more passion than we hold our love of God and of others. In many ways, this is the central message of Schleiermacher.

MUSINGS

How have you seen disputes over doctrine become divisive to those around you?

How have you seen these disputes play out in your own life?

What step can you take today to replace love of doctrine with love of God?

DAY 14

EVOLUTION

"...for the merely gradual and imperfect unfolding of the power of God-consciousness is one of the necessary conditions of the human stage of existence."

— Friedrich Schleiermacher
The Christian Faith

WE ARE IMPERFECT BEINGS. Part of that imperfection comes from a lack of knowledge and awareness of the realities around us.

We are constantly learning...constantly growing...constantly changing...constantly evolving. Literally and figuratively, we are not the same person we were five minutes ago!

This evolution extends to what Schleiermacher called our God-consciousness. We may live in a state where we do not see or acknowledge God around us. Or we may be in a place where we richly experience fellowship with the Divine. In either circumstance, our knowledge is incomplete. As the Apostle Paul put it, "For now we see only a reflection as in a mirror" (I Corinthians 13:12a).

It is a necessary condition of our humanity to lack a full understanding of who God is. As such, it is important to give each other both the grace and the space in our own journeys of discovery.

May today be a day of respectful empathy towards others and growth for yourself. Embrace the wonder of the process. Embrace your personal evolution.

MUSINGS

Describe one way in which you've changed over this past year.

How may it be freeing for you to realize that you are evolving, and that is ok?

How can this realization impact your view of others around you?

DAY 15

FATHER OF HERMENEUTICS

"The task [of hermeneutics] is also to be expressed as follows,
to understand the utterance at first just as well, and then better,
than its author."

— Friedrich Schleiermacher
Hermeneutics and Criticism

SCHLEIERMACHER IS NOT ONLY known as the Father of Modern Theology
but also as the Father of Modern Hermeneutics. This is because he was the
first to propose general rules for interpretation, which broadened hermeneutics to the study of understanding itself. He created a new discipline by
providing a universal set of guidelines for the interpretive task.

Key among Schleiermacher's principles is that there is no 'objective' or
'plain reading' of any text. If we claim that we are reading something 'literally'
on its face, we are misreading it. To get to the true meaning of what is
written, we must account for several variables: culture, linguistics, personal
experience, social norms and biases, etc.

We naturally read ourselves into a text, and we mustn't allow this to occur.
Schleiermacher felt that the natural course of reading was to misunderstand

(at least in some way) the author's meaning. The cure for this was the application of hermeneutic principles. It was both an art and a science.

What's more, when writing, an author may be unaware of her own impulses and biases. For this reason, Schleiermacher felt the interpreter must be able to understand a text better than the author herself.

Meaning transcends authorship...and we have Schleiermacher to thank for this realization.

MUSINGS

How does our reading of any work become skewed without the application of hermeneutic principles?

How can this impact our reading of the Bible?

How can hermeneutics impact your understanding of God?

DAY 16

BIBLICISM

"The New Testament has obtained its present form through
the decision of the church...This is not a decision to which we
attribute an authority exalted above all inquiry, and thus we
are quite justified in starting fresh investigations in connection
with earlier waverings on the boundary."

— Friedrich Schleiermacher
Brief Outline of Theology as a Field of Study

THE COMMON DEFINITION OF biblicism is the acceptance of and adherence
to the letter of the Bible. Schleiermacher viewed the Bible to be informative
and even foundational for the practice of the Christian faith, but he did not
believe the authority of everything contained within the Canon to be beyond
question.

Though commonly understood as such, the Bible is not the
word-for-word dictation of God to man. It is a text compiled over centuries,
authored by many, and varied in its presentation of histories and insights. We
must not mistake 'inspired' for 'infallible.'

From Schleiermacher's perspective, Christians grant authority to the Bible because of their faith in Christ. They do not believe in Christ because of their faith in the Bible. Put differently, the Bible informs faith, it is not the foundation of it.

Let us embrace the Sacred Text for the wonder of wisdom and truth it contains. But we must never do so blindly or thoughtlessly. Fundamentalism only leads to rule-following. But in having the heart of a seeker, one will discover the depths of companionship with the Divine.

MUSINGS

How does today's reading resonate with you?

How would you describe your current view of biblical authority or inspiration?

How might your relationship with God change by viewing the Bible as a diversely-written text?

DAY 17

FREEDOM IN DEPENDENCE

"Those who can imagine a God who performs acts of self-limitation can also flatter themselves into believing in a freedom that raises itself above absolute dependence."

— Friedrich Schleiermacher
On the Glaubenslehre

WE ARE A FREE people. We relish our liberties, and we shun restraint. We are often tempted to do something simply because it is the opposite of what we are told. This isn't, of course, an inherently wrong approach to take. It's natural to doubt the sincerity and wisdom of others above our own inclinations.

But what if there was someone who was all-wise, all-loving, and motivated by nothing other than seeing our best come to fruition? And what if that same person went all-in every moment of every day, not even sparing themselves to see that end come to pass?

For Schleiermacher, that person was God. The Father of Modern Theology continuously sought after God and recognized that he was only as free as he was willing to be dependent on the One who knew what was best for him.

Our proclivities toward stubbornness should never be underestimated. But obstinance leads only to our detriment when we refuse to defer to God's guidance.

May we find the strength to change course when those inclinations arise. May we find true liberation in the freedom that comes from being absolutely dependent on God.

MUSINGS

What is your initial reaction when you are asked to be dependent on something or someone?

Why is it hard for us to allow ourselves to depend on anything?

What step can you take today to allow yourself to be dependent on God?

DAY 18

CONVERTS

"As I myself have willingly confessed, the endeavor to make proselytes from unbelievers is deep-rooted in religion. Yet that is not what now urges me to speak to you."

— Friedrich Schleiermacher
On Religion

WHEN WE BELIEVE SOMETHING with all our hearts, especially if that thing brings us hope, we want to share it with others. As suggested above, it is a 'deep-rooted' inclination. This is a good thing. We are motivated to love others because we have discovered the One who first loved us (1 John 4:19). But this is not the source of Schleiermacher's admission.

In the opening lines of the third of his speeches *On Religion*, Schleiermacher is reflecting on his years with the deeply pious Moravian community. The Moravians committed their lives to the proselytization of the Christian faith, at times even selling themselves into slavery to reach remote tribes and create converts.

In today's reading, Schleiermacher is not condemning the mission, but he *is* denouncing the 'motion.' The distinction is noteworthy.

As Christians, we can be so dedicated to 'saving souls' that we argue, debate, and even sell ourselves to convince others to turn from their wicked ways. We are driven to assure the multitudes' place in heaven while storing up treasures there for ourselves.

But barely twenty years of age, Schleiermacher had already discovered such motivations are ineffective in causing true and lasting change. He had found it best to simply speak from the heart, to share Love from a place of love. And in doing so, he penned a work that has been read for over 200 years and which is considered the first major writing of the Father of Modern Theology.

Christianity is at its best when it is more concerned with loving others than with accomplishing an agenda. Let us be agents of that great Love. There is no surer way for eyes to be open than when others can see the heart of God through our own.

MUSINGS

Describe a time when you were motivated to change someone's mind instead of loving them.

Can lasting change come from a place other than love? Why or why not?

Who is someone who needs your love today? How will you show it to them?

DAY 19

PARTING WAYS

"The law of reason can never
determine our will immediately."

— Friedrich Schleiermacher
The Highest Good

SCHLEIERMACHER AND IMMANUEL KANT were contemporaries, though Kant was Schleiermacher's senior. They even met on one occasion.

Young Schleiermacher was initially enthralled with the writings of Kant. Schleiermacher's curiosity about the rising philosophy star even got him in trouble while attending the strict Moravian Pietist school to which his father sent him.

In the Moravian community, what was allowed to be read was hand-picked. Banned were the writings of 'worldly' perspectives. But young Friedrich didn't seem to care. He would sneak in books by the dark of night simply to read and to learn. That the teachings within these volumes were forbidden made the learning all the more exciting. One day, the rebellious teen got caught red-handed reading Kant's *Critique of Practical Reason*, an affair that nearly resulted in his expulsion.

No matter, Schleiermacher would soon successfully petition his father to allow him to quit and attend Germany's University of Halle. But as Schleiermacher continued to read Kant as well as develop his own philosophical brass, he began to find several points of disagreement with the man he admired.

Perhaps primary among them was Kant's assertion that what is moral can ultimately be determined through pure reason. It was during that time, in Schleiermacher's early twenties, that he was beginning to develop his philosophy of *Gefühl* (or "feeling"). What would go on to become his terminology for the immediate self-consciousness of God, in fact, began as a term to denote a 'dispassionate gentleness' that guided our moral inclinations.

For Schleiermacher, reason alone was an insufficient guide for moral choice. *Gefühl*, instead, served to be a subconscious faculty aiding moral man. As it developed, moral choices became easier. Without it, man was left ill-equipped to determine right action.

Schleiermacher would spend much of his career rebutting Kantian principles in light of *Gefühl*, but it all started with a schoolboy's infatuation with that very adversary.

Likewise, may we be willing to part ways with those whom we have previously given a position of authority when our experience has outgrown their tutelage.

MUSINGS

How does today's reading resonate with you?

What relationship in your life have you perhaps outgrown?

How might you need to define that relationship moving forward?

DAY 20

UNDAUNTED

"Even less can I acknowledge an obligation to refute objections which in my opinion miss the point or are based on misunderstandings. An author does not owe this to the critics, who deal with the subject matter all the time and therefore can come to their own conclusions."

— **Friedrich Schleiermacher**
On the Glaubenslehre

THE RADICAL REFRAMING OF religion Schleiermacher provided, in response to the attempts by Enlightenment thinkers to dismantle and discard it, was not without its own critics.

Spurning past orthodoxies, the Father of Modern Theology would undergird his approach to religion, not in static dogmas or tired tradition, but in feeling. More specifically, the 'feeling of absolute dependence on God.'

Among his most vocal critics was German philosopher G. W. Hegel, who famously chided, "If religion is based on a feeling...then a dog would be the best Christian since a dog is most strongly characterized by this feeling and lives primarily in this feeling."

This was not only a gross misrepresentation of Schleiermacher's philosophy, but also a personal blow, as Schleiermacher had been instrumental in bringing Hegel to the University of Berlin (a university for which he was a founding member).

Nonetheless, Schleiermacher persisted.

And when Hegel founded the Society for Scientific Criticism largely to counter the messages of Schleiermacher's Academy of Sciences, Schleiermacher continued, undaunted.

Schleiermacher realized that criticism is often just a sign that one is pushing against stubborn grain. And he would go on to plow a path that would be trodden by generations to come.

Never let your critics change your message. Remember that the only taste of success some people will ever have is when they take a bite out of you.

MUSINGS

Describe a time when you were frustrated by the criticism of others.

How did you handle this criticism?

What does 'continuing undaunted' mean for you this morning, as you begin your day?

DAY 21

PRUDENCE

Wherever fruit appears as the spontaneous result of your life's free flowering, let it develop to the world's advantage...But let whatever you offer to the world be fruit. Do not sacrifice the least part of your being itself in mistaken generosity! Let no bud be broken off, nor the smallest leaf plucked, through which you receive nourishment from the world around you."

— **Friedrich Schleiermacher**
The Monologen

WE ARE ONLY AS valuable to those around us as we are healthy ourselves. It is okay, even necessary, to tend to our own needs before helping others.

As believers in a God who gave so that we could be whole, it is vital to realize, though His body was broken, He gave from a place of completeness.

Jesus was no less God on the cross than off of it.

We needn't feel that following in the footsteps of Christ means self-abnegation. When we sense that we have no fruit to bear, in those times, we need to let ourselves be nourished by those who do.

Once whole, we can offer the fruits of our healing to others who may need it.

It benefits no one to give our broken buds and withered leaves. It is dangerous to both the one who gives and the one given to.

May you grace yourself today with the permission to stop, to rest, and to receive from others if that's what you need. May your life be marked by seasons of giving and receiving, and the prudence to know the difference.

MUSINGS

Have you ever tried to give from a place of brokenness? What was the result?

Who in your life can you look to when you are feeling broken?

How can you depend on God today for wholeness?

DAY 22

LOVE AND MORALITY

"Not recognizing its sacredness, they cast it carelessly into the common pool of human goods, that should be governed according to universal law. But for us, O love,
thou art alpha and omega."

— Friedrich Schleiermacher
The Monologen

SCHLEIERMACHER WAS OBSESSED WITH the writings of Immanuel Kant during his time in secondary school and university. But he would eventually find many points of departure from his former philosophic muse.

Among them was the rejection of Kant's Categorical Imperative, or the idea that what is moral is not dependent upon circumstance, but binding for all occasions. For Schleiermacher, however, morality was linked inextricably to the individual, and to time and context.

Ultimately, he felt we must be driven, not by the rule of law, but by the law of love.

If who we are and what we do are centered in love, we will always act in a way that is morally sound.

Let Love be your muse, your guide and your ultimate aim today.

Life deprived of love is deprived of meaning. But with love, the Universe stands within your grasp.

MUSINGS

What helps you determine what is right when you are uncertain how to act in a situation?

What does 'living from a place of love' mean for you?

How can acting in love change a circumstance you find yourself facing today?

DAY 23

The Spark

"But wherever I do see a spark of the hidden fire that must sooner or later consume the outworn and recreate the world, I am drawn toward it with love and true hope as a welcome sign of my distant home."

— Friedrich Schleiermacher
The Monologen

In Schleiermacher's third monologue, he laments those who pass "from hope in life to contempt for it." When our focus is on external circumstances, it is easy to become sad, disappointed, and even jaded.

He contrasts this state with the one who is able to live in "the way of beauty." To them, "belongs to a world that is yet to be."

The difference between the two is not the false hope of escapism, nor is it personal striving. For Schleiermacher, the one who is able to truly live is she who is able to cultivate community. For the young philosopher, life is best when "friends extend to each other the hand of fellowship," for "the bond [results] in something greater than each could achieve independently."

We are at our greatest when we exist in togetherness. When we show sympathy, exchange knowledge, and mitigate suffering, independence becomes a mere illusion, and interdependence is our high calling.

May we realize today that we are relational beings, designed for life in community, with God, and with others. May we create a world for ourselves in which the fire of our interconnectedness consumes us.

And may we then be the Spark to inspire the same in someone else.

MUSINGS

Who do you consider 'your community'?

What step can you take today to deepen your relationship with them?

If God is a relational Being, how might God become a part of your community?

DAY 24

REGARDLESS

"I confidently greet the future...I am its master, it is not mine."

— Friedrich Schleiermacher
The Monologen

SCHLEIERMACHER STRONGLY BELIEVED THAT the most important part of life was found in the inner self and not outer circumstances.

With his own homeland besieged by the armies of Napoleon, Schleiermacher was not a stranger to loss, uncertainty, or shifting fortunes. One can control what happens around them little more than they can dictate the movement of the planets above.

But, for the Father of Modern Theology, it was not outward events that determined his inward peace. If it were, calmness would come and go with the tameless tides of time.

No, lasting peace would only be found by peering inward and the cultivation of the spiritual life. There man meets God, the temporal collides with the timeless, and the decaying finds respite in the imperishable.

When we find this peace, we can truly be the master of our own future, for what happens can no longer rob us of our tranquility. Obstacles become mere opportunities to develop this feeling further.

May you find this peace today. And may it remain ever with you. Not because of what your day will bring, but regardless.

MUSINGS

What 'outer circumstances' are causing you distress?

How can focusing on the spiritual help you cope with these stresses?

How can you take a meaningful step today to cultivate growth in your spiritual life?

DAY 25

IMMORTALITY

"In such terms, men have also tried to imagine immortality,
but all too content with the earthly life, they aspire to it only
after death."

— Friedrich Schleiermacher
The Monologen

IT IS COMMON FOR us to desire things we don't have. It seems that most
of our time is spent striving to achieve the next best thing so that we may
someday find satisfaction in surrounding circumstances.

We resign ourselves to such an existence, convinced that the model of the
world is also an adequate prescription for our lives. Certain that the best is
only ahead of us, we find contentment in running the race.

We even do this as Christians. We place our hope in a future immortality
and never realize that such a gift is ours today. There is nothing available to
us after death that cannot be experienced in the present.

Peace. Rest. Joy. Communion with God. Inner contentment regardless of
external uncertainty. These are all ours for the taking.

We need not content ourselves with the shallow solace of temporal hope. Realize today your immortality.

MUSINGS

What comes to mind when you hear the term 'immortality'?

What are you currently striving towards that is causing delayed contentment?

How would your life be different if you embraced immortality?

DAY 26

COMMUNITY

"The Christian church is a community,...in such a way that
each individual is affected by the whole and understands himself only in terms of the whole."

— Friedrich Schleiermacher
Introduction to Christian Ethics

WE LIVE IN A culture that prioritizes individuality. In many important ways,
this is a great thing. No two people are exactly alike. We are uniquely made.
We have unique talents, and we possess unique passions, priorities, and perspectives. This should be rightfully celebrated.

But, as a theologian and pastor, Schleiermacher understood that individuality does not necessitate isolation. In fact, for as much as we are remarkable,
we are also relational. We thrive when we are an integrated part of a larger
community, and we suffer in separation.

This is especially true for the body of believers known as the Church.
United by the redemptive work of Christ, we are one in our desire to experience God's love and live in such a way that others experience that love
through us.

No decision is made by one that does not affect the whole. No success can be celebrated, nor sin sequestered, apart from the larger body.

When we realize our inherent oneness, we begin to see God as easily by 'looking around' as we do by 'looking up.'

Let us embrace this truth today: we can only pursue our purpose as we cultivate community.

MUSINGS

Have you ever mistaken isolation for individuality? How can we be in community and still remain true to ourselves?

In what ways are we not able to fulfill our purpose outside of life in community?

How might it be easier to experience God when we are close to other people?

DAY 27

WE INTUIT GOD

"The feeling of absolute dependence...is a universal element
of life; and the recognition of this fact entirely takes the place,
for the system of doctrine, of all the so-called proofs of the
existence of God."

— **Friedrich Schleiermacher**
The Christin Faith

I HAVE READ MANY arguments for God's existence (the moral argument, the
argument from logic, the ontological argument, and many more.) For me, it
is the experience of God that is the most convincing. Call it the 'argument
from individual intuition.'

At its most basic level, Schleiermacher calls this experience of God 'a
taste for the infinite.' As it develops, he refers to it as a 'feeling of absolute
dependence.'

It is not a subjective feeling Schleiermacher references here. This feeling
can be likened to the feeling we have of our eyes in our sockets or the brain
in our head. Non-sensate, but instinctual.

Do we have any confirmation that we intuit God?

I would say yes. Religious experience has been a part of culture from the development of mankind. The explanations and details change but the 'taste for the infinite' in our finitude remains unchanged.

It is this experience Schleiermacher says takes the place of all 'so-called proofs of the existence of God.'

Confidence in God's existence is the doorway to the fruits of a relationship with God. May such confidence be yours to enjoy today.

MUSINGS

Have you ever doubted the existence of God? What arguments, if any, have you found helpful?

Do you agree with the suggestion that we all intuit the existence of God? Why or why not?

Schleiermacher calls our intuition of God a 'taste for the infinite.' What does that phrase mean to you?

DAY 28

INSPIRATION

"I have spent the greater part of the forenoon in arranging my head an introduction to one of Plato's dialogues. I would willingly have discarded the subject and sat down at once to chat with you, but I felt that I ought not to do so.

Most people think me an extraordinary being who can do everything he wills to do, and whenever he wills to do it...But the fact is, that my case is exactly the contrary. I can do nothing, absolutely nothing, by mere force of will, but must await the favorable moment. Therefore, when it comes, I should consider myself very culpable were I to let it pass without availing myself to it."

— Friedrich Schleiermacher
Personal Letters

THE FATHER OF MODERN Theology was a true polymath. He was a preacher, professor, author of volumes of work, translator of Aristotle and Plato, and much more. However, as the above letter written to his future wife demonstrates, even he considered himself a slave to moments of inspiration.

We all have goals. We all have lists of achievements we would consider within our reach if the right moment simply collided with proper motivation. Whether it be a career change, a matter of physical health, relational success, or a new avenue of financial gain, Creativity must be cultivated before progress can be pursued.

At times, those moments come organically. When they do, we must embrace them with our whole being. But Schleiermacher also knew where these occasions originated and upon Whom he needed to rely when he experienced prolonged intervals of inactivity.

For him, the essence of religion itself was the 'feeling of absolute dependence' one must develop toward the Divine. Once realized, he felt freedom could be truly experienced. We could live as we ought to live, and success could be seen as areas of opportunity become periods of prosperity.

May we recognize today that this dependence is the source of our desired inspiration. And when those moments of motivation arise, may we dare not let them pass.

MUSINGS

What goal(s) would you like to accomplish, if only you could find the inspiration?

Where have you found inspiration in your life?

What does it mean to you to recognize your dependence on God?

DAY 29

Inclusivism

"It matters not what conceptions a man adheres to, he can still be pious. His piety, the divine in his feeling, may be better than his conception, and his desire to place the essence of his piety in conception only makes him misunderstand himself."

— Friedrich Schleiermacher
On Religion

THE GREAT ENLIGHTENMENT WAS a period of deconstruction in religion. Reason was handed the seat of authority, and all other avenues of truth were either minimized or neglected.

Piety (or sincere devotion to faith) was subject to rationalism's assault, as concepts of God were being forced to fit into boxes designed by the logic of humanity.

In his second speech *On Religion*, Schleiermacher rebukes these 'cultured despisers' of religion and insists they are missing the point. For him, religion was not based in the doctrines or dogmas of reason, but in God-inspired feeling. He would go on to say that the essence of religion itself is the 'feeling' of absolute dependence on God.

Not that reason wasn't a useful tool to discover truths regarding God, but 'knowledge about' God is very different than 'devotion to' God.

Though we are now living in postmodern times, there are lessons to be learned from the battles Schleiermacher fought over 200 years ago.

We can easily see followers of faiths that aren't ours as simply wrong or misguided. We criticize and make them objects of argument, instead of recognizing them as sincere seekers. We critique their conclusions instead of acknowledging the Source of their piety is no different than that of our own.

Differences are always worth discussing, but we are off base when we start from a place of judgment rather than God-infused love.

Knowledge can never be the measure of piety. If it were, we would all be subject to an impossible standard.

Let us hold loosely to our dogmatic formulas today as we hold tightly to our love for God and humanity around us.

MUSINGS

What does the phrase 'knowledge can never be a measure of piety' mean to you?

Describe a time in your life in which you valued dogmatic formula over love?

How would you look at people differently if you recognized they were sincere seekers of truth?

DAY 30

GOD OF ALL

"Man is born with the religious capacity as with any other. If
only his sense for the profoundest depths of his own nature
is not crushed out, if only all fellowship between himself and
the Primal Source is not quite shut off, religion would, after
its own fashion, infallibly be developed."

— Friedrich Schleiermacher
On Religion

ONE OF RELIGION'S MOST effective deterrents is the damage that has been
inflicted on its behalf. War, persecution, and discrimination are just a few of
the blights which stain the long history of egregious errors perpetrated in the
name of faith.

In many ways worse than these, however, is the common claim that only
some are chosen by God to know God. The argument goes something along
the lines of, "God is sovereign, and His will cannot be resisted. Those who
do not know God were never meant to in the first place." Hogwash.

As Creator and Sustainer of all things, God loves creation and continuously draws and woos all to deeper and deeper relationship. And as beings

fashioned in God's image, we all have the capacity to gain a sense of the presence and calling of God.

Schleiermacher's admonition in the above quote is to those people and circumstances who would serve to 'crush out' humanity's inclination towards the Divine.

May we realize today that God is a God who is for all. May our life's aim be to foster this sense in ourselves and for others.

There is no greater purpose in life than to respond to this call.

MUSINGS

Describe a time when your actions have served to inspire others toward belief?

Describe a time when your actions served to crush belief out?

How might your worldview change by realizing God is a God 'for all'?

FATHER OF MODERN THEOLOGY
An Introduction to THE MONOLOGEN

AN ENLIGHTENED AGE

THE AGE OF ENLIGHTENMENT was a period spanning from 1685 to 1815. This time's vast intellectual and scientific progress was ignited as past orthodoxies were spurned. German philosopher Immanuel Kant defined the motivating force behind Enlightenment thinking as humankind's desire to be released from "self-inflicted immaturity," which he said was demonstrated by the "inability to use one's own understanding without the guidance of another."[1] In the Enlightenment, ultimate confidence was placed in the individual's capacity to reason her way to truth, independent of the crutches of tradition, authority, or superstition.

The implications for religious orthodoxy were apparent. The Church, the Bible, and even the faith community were no longer seen as the wellsprings of wisdom they had once been. Natural religion became the predominant means of attaining knowledge about God. Reason, sense perception, and introspection were the only reliable tools at hand. Findings not limited to utilizing these methods were dismissed a priori. As such, most forms of Christian theism became seen as anti-intellectual and, therefore, baseless as part of the larger pursuit of certitude.

Immanuel Kant and Scottish philosopher David Hume were two thought leaders whose writings became emblematic of the Enlightenment. Their responses to the precepts of natural religion were to influence generations as well as set the stage for the entrance of the novel ideas of the man who would become known as the Father of Modern Theology, Friedrich Schleiermacher.

KANT'S MORAL THEISM

For Immanuel Kant, moral living was a self-sufficient good. In the preface to his book *Religion within the Boundaries of Mere Reason*, Kant writes:

> "So far as morality is based on the concept of the human being as one who...binds himself through his reason to unconditional laws, it is in need neither of the idea of another being above him to recognize his duty, nor that he observe it, [as] an incentive other than the law itself."[2]

For Kant, the precepts of moral law that bind us are available from practical reason and need not be revealed through divine intervention. Kant's formulation of the 'highest good' was achieved in putting into practice what he famously dubbed 'the categorical imperative,' that we should "act only in accordance with that maxim through which you can at the same time will that it become universal law."[3] In other words, we must do good because we have reasoned the act to be good in and of itself. Kant rejected a priori the hierarchy of the established church, the traditional practices of worship and prayer, miracles, the primacy of Christianity, and belief in the divine inspiration of the Bible. They served no purpose. He called them "religious delusions and counterfeit services to God."[4]

With that said, belief in God was necessary for Kant, if only to ground moral practice. He reasoned that it was natural to ask "to what end" our moral behavior was in service to the highest good. We can act charitably or with compassion, but will our actions result in proportional happiness? To achieve such confidence, a higher power must exist. In his words:

"If the strictest observance of the moral laws is to be thought of as the cause of the ushering in of the highest good, then, since human capacity does not suffice to effect happiness in the world...an omnipotent moral being must be assumed as the ruler of the world, under whose care this would come about...morality inevitably leads to religion."[5]

For Kant, morality took priority over religion but also led to religion, which was necessary when the ultimate end of our actions was considered. Religion justified faith in the culmination of the highest good.

Giving primacy to morality also allowed Kant to postulate immortality. He went as far as to suggest belief in immortality was "morally necessary."[6] Kant believed if God did not exist and morality could not be realized posthumously, "then the moral law, which commands that it be furthered, must be fantastic, directed to empty, imaginary ends, and consequently inherently false."[7]

HUME'S RADICAL EMPIRICISM

If Kant wanted to relegate belief in God to the sphere of moral behavior, David Hume desired to banish belief in the divine altogether. In his *Dialogues on Natural Religion*, Hume referenced an illustration used to demonstrate the futility of the search for the ultimate ground of reality. "Let us remember the story of the Indian philosopher and his elephant," Hume wrote.[8] In this story, the philosopher's disciple inquires what it was that the world rests upon. The philosopher replies the world rests upon the back of an elephant. The disciple then asks what the elephant rests on, and the philosopher states the elephant rests on the back of a tortoise. When the student asks what it was that supports the tortoise, the philosopher replies, "I know not what." Hume insisted it was impossible to use reason to obtain knowledge.

Instead, Hume believed there were only two sources of truth: the abstract ideas of mathematics and logic, and contingent propositions concerning matters of fact.[9] And the latter can only be affirmed through experience. Illustrations of Hume's radical empiricism included the proposition that we could not conclusively say any succession of events occurred through cause and effect, or even that the chairs we sit in exist independently and will continue to exist once we walk out of the room. We can know only that which we experience. And we can expect to be true only that which our experiences intuit.

It is not hard to deduce, then, how Hume felt about the matters of religion. Hume left very little room for justification of belief in God. Even less room for the occurrence of the miraculous. In his *Inquiry Concerning Human Understanding*, Hume observed that a miracle, by definition, is "a violation of the laws of nature; and as a firm and unalterable experience has established these laws, the proof against a miracle, from the very nature of fact, is as entire as any argument from experience can possibly be imagined."[10] Hume went on to quip that proof for a miracle would need to be so strong that "its falsehood would be more miraculous than the fact which it endeavors to establish."[11] Hume's opposition to religion was so vigorous that on his deathbed, he declared the only reason he should want to remain alive was that he had, "been endeavoring to open the eyes of the public. If I should live a few years longer, I may have the satisfaction of seeing the downfall of some of the prevailing systems of superstition...till I have the pleasure of seeing the churches shut up and the clergy sent about their business."[12]

With Kant and Hume emblematic of the Enlightenment's deconstruction of religious orthodoxy, faith took a backseat to intellectual progress. Friedrich Schleiermacher, a child of Enlightenment, would set his eyes on responding to these 'cultured despisers' of religion. In doing so, he would dramatically reframe faith as he attempted to marry Enlightenment thinking to a Christian framework.

UPBRINGING OF THE FATHER
OF MODERN THEOLOGY

To understand Schleiermacher's approach to Enlightenment thinking, in general, and the Christian faith, specifically, it is essential to view them in light of his formative years. Friedrich Daniel Ernst Schleiermacher was born in 1768 in Breslau (modern-day Wroclaw, Poland) to Gottlieb Schleiermacher, a Reformed Church chaplain in the Prussian Army. Friedrich would eventually become the third in a line of Reformed pastors, as Gottlieb's father was also one.

Schleiermacher's early years were pivotal in his theological and philosophic development. When he was fourteen years old, he was sent by his father to live within the Moravian community. The Moravians were known for their focus on the experience of faith. For them, personal piety and inner transformation were central to the Christian life. They were committed to continual, uninterrupted prayer, an achievement that lasted for over one hundred years. And they were so dedicated to missions that they were known to have sold themselves into slavery to reach the lost in unevangelized regions of the world. These passions and proclivities would remain hallmarks of Schleiermacher's writings and ministry throughout his life.[13]

Schleiermacher left the community at seventeen to attend a Moravian theological school in Barby, Germany. The school was strict and only allowed its students to read approved materials. A book was not permitted onsite if it did not meet Moravian standards. This left the inquisitive Schleiermacher unsatisfied, as he knew of the cultural revolution outside the academy's walls. Schleiermacher would often sneak in banned books, reading forbidden literature by the dark of night. One encounter left the enthusiastic student nearly expelled as he was caught holding a copy of Immanuel Kant's *Critique of Practical Reason*.

Needless to say, Schleiermacher was left intellectually unfulfilled at Barby. It was a strict institution with little tolerance for a doubter's questions, so Friedrich found himself in sharp personal conflict. He had grown to be uncertain regarding dogmas central to Moravian thought. He questioned ideas such as the divinity of Christ and the necessity of a blood atonement. At nineteen, he would successfully petition his father to leave Barby and continue his education at the University of Halle. Still, the importance of Schleiermacher's time with the Moravians and the experience of the pious life cannot be overstated. As he would go on to reflect:

> "Here my consciousness of the relation of human beings to a higher world first arose…Here there first developed the mystical disposition which is so essential to me and has saved and preserved me under all the assaults of skepticism."[14]

At Halle, Schleiermacher found his passions in ancient literature and philosophy. He worked on translating Aristotle's *Ethics* into the German tongue and would eventually translate Plato's major works. Even so, Kant remained Schleiermacher's philosophic obsession.[15] For Kant, reason was not to be found in external structures of the physical world or the practices of tradition. Inner reason received primacy, and evaluation of this concept became a driving force behind Schleiermacher's schema. His deconstruction of past beliefs led to great uncertainty. Schleiermacher was still driven towards ministry, but now he was skeptical that the religion he held onto could benefit others. At one particularly low point, the young student grew depressed and even discussed the merits of suicide with a close friend.[16]

In 1790, Schleiermacher accepted a position as a tutor in the house of Count Dohna in East Prussia. This appointment would prove lifesaving for the new graduate. In his words, "In a stranger's home, my sense for the beauty of human fellowship was awakened; I saw that it takes freedom to ennoble and give right expression to the delicate intimacies of human nature."[17] Here, too, Schleiermacher had his first experience of love, in the form of an unspoken passion for the daughter of the Count. It would be the personal encounters at Dohna's estate, not philosophy, which would rekindle his love for God and humanity.

Schleiermacher would go on in 1793 to become a preacher and teacher at a large school for orphans in Berlin, and then in 1796 to be appointed as chaplain for the Reformed Confession in a prominent Berlin hospital. During this time, Schleiermacher met Friedrich Schlegel (who was to become a key founder of German Romanticism) in a salon which they both frequented. They often met, sharing their mutual passion for Greek literature and the ideals of beauty, love, and nature. Already an accomplished author, Schlegel continually encouraged Schleiermacher to write. This prodding resulted in the publication of what was to become one of the future scholar's most significant and impactful achievements, "*On Religion: Speeches to its Cultured Despisers*."[18]

Schleiermacher's conception of what religion was had matured. As Enlightenment thinking dismantled the trophies of orthodoxy and biblicism, his Moravian roots remained[19] and served as a basis for the infusion of Romantic ideals. For Schleiermacher, piety had become "neither a Knowing nor a Doing, but a modification of Feeling."[20] And on that foundation, Schleiermacher would frame the essence of religion as the "feeling of absolute dependence on God."[21] Further, this essence, he determined, "was not an accidental element, or thing which varies from person to person, but a universal element of life." Indeed, for Schleiermacher:

> "Man is born with the religious capacity as with every other.
> If only his sense for the profoundest depths of his own nature
> is not crushed out, if only all fellowship between himself and
> the Primal Source is not quite shut off, religion would, after
> its own fashion, infallibly be developed."[22]

Achieving a philosophy based on sense and experience would become his primary point of departure from the man whose writing had served to be so formative for him. As he would set his sights on Immanuel Kant, Schleiermacher would create a pathway that would not only provide the groundwork for his eventual christening as the Father of Modern Theology but also dull the necessary appeal to a tired orthodoxy, which had been critical to the Enlightenment's assault on religion.

A PHILOSOPHER OF FEELING

No term is more misunderstood, yet central to the theology of Schleiermacher, as *Gefühl* ("feeling"). For some critics, *Gefühl's* usage as a grounding principle meant that faith was subjective and left up to personal interpretation. For others, it meant belief was to be driven primarily by emotion, subject to whimsical change. But such notions were far from Schleiermacher's intention, and the development of his usage of *Gefühl* paints a much different picture.

When Schleiermacher was in his twenties and struggling to make sense of the faith of his youth, he found a home in the study of philosophy. It was in the late 1780s that *Gefühl* began to emerge as an important concept, becoming a central theme in the area of ethics, aesthetics, and more. However, Schleiermacher's appropriation of the term would be unique among his contemporaries. We first find Schleiermacher using *Gefühl* as a mode of moral discernment in 1788 in his earliest surviving essay, *Notes on Aristotle*.[23] In this essay, *Gefühl* is a nurturing agent, leading the subject to the "better feelings" of a refined character.[24] In 1789, Schleiermacher used *Gefühl* in his response to Kant's "Critique of Practical Reason," *On the Highest Good*. Here, *Gefühl* becomes a faculty of moral discernment. It is a guiding light. Not in any way emotional, Schleiermacher calls *Gefühl* a "dispassionate gentleness."[25]

As Schleiermacher continued to study works of past and contemporary philosophy, he refined his usage of *Gefühl* further. In his 1792 essay, *On Freedom*, Schleiermacher honed in more closely on Kant, using *Gefühl* to denote the capacity to know and act upon a situation's highest good.[26] For Schleiermacher, *Gefühl* accomplishes the work that reason alone is incapable of doing.

In 1799, Schleiermacher's usage of *Gefühl* began to reach maturity. As his passion for faith became rekindled, Schleiermacher would utilize *Gefühl* as the foundational principle of religion itself. Enlightenment thinking sought to reason away the need for belief in anything other than the accomplishments of humanity. Kant had sought to establish morality in that very same capacity for reason. In his landmark defense of religion, Schleiermacher would argue both these sentiments miss the point. He would admonish:

> "Religion is for you at one time a way of thinking...a particular way to contemplate the world, [as well as] a way of acting...a special kind of conduct and character...I consider it very wrong that out of things so disparate as modes of knowing and modes of acting, you patch together an untenable something, and call it religion."[27]

Instead, for Schleiermacher:

> "The contemplation of the pious is the immediate self-consciousness of the universal existence of all finite things, in and through the Infinite, and all temporal things in and through the Eternal. *Religion is to seek this and find it in all that lives and moves...It is to have life and to know life in immediate feeling* [*Gefühl*], *only as such an existence in the Infinite and Eternal.*"[28] (emphasis mine)

By grounding the essence of religion in *Gefühl*, Schleiermacher would realize two key achievements that cannot be understated. First and foremost, he offered an apologetic for faith. One that had remained untouched by Enlightenment deconstruction. He would profess in his 1821 dogmatics work, *The Christian Faith*, that "the recognition of this [feeling] entirely takes the place, for the system of doctrine, of all the so-called proofs of the existence of God."[29] Secondly, Schleiermacher recentered faith. No longer was the believer to look "up there somewhere" for the Divine. God was most readily found by looking inward to where God was experienced. This was not at all a feeling in the sense of sentiment or emotion, but an inclination located in what Schleiermacher called the "immediate self-consciousness." For the first time, religion was not framed in the happenings of history, the dogmas of the Church, or the trappings of tradition. It was centered on the experience of the believer. Schleiermacher would summarize what he deemed the true foundation of religion to be:

> "The common element in all howsoever diverse expressions of piety, by which these are conjointly distinguished from all other feelings...is this: the consciousness of being absolutely dependent, or which is the same thing, of being in relation with God."[30]

The tectonic shift Schleiermacher would initiate for the centering principles of religion would cause him to later be known as the Father of Modern Theology. At the same time, it would also make him a lightning rod for criticism. One of Schleiermacher's most prolific critics, Karl Barth would opine:

> "If feeling is the essential organ of religion, the nature of God is nothing else than an expression of the nature of feeling...the object of religious feeling is become a matter of indifference. Once feeling has been pronounced the subjective essence of religion, it in fact is also the objective essence...feeling is pronounced to be religious, simply because it is feeling."[31]

The most famous criticism came from philosopher and contemporary rival G. W. Hegel:

"Should feeling constitute the basic determination of human nature, then humans are equated with animals, for feeling is what is specific to animals...If religion in humans is based on feeling...then a dog would be the best Christian, since a dog is most strongly characterized by...feeling and lives predominantly in this feeling."[32]

Schleiermacher was aware of Hegel's critique but was undaunted by it. *Gefühl* did not have its origin in the subjectivity of base emotion but in the 'immediate self-consciousness.' Of course, what he meant by that phrase would need further clarification. And as Schleiermacher's theological and philosophic prowess continued to mature, he would further develop exactly what takes place at the convergence of 'consciousness' and *Gefühl*. In doing so, he would provide a pathway to overcome what he saw as another Kantian error, the separation of body and mind found in his advocacy of dualism.

SCHLEIERMACHER OFFERS AN ALTERNATIVE TO KANTIAN DUALISM

Among the growing points of departure from Kantian philosophy was the philosophical system Schleiermacher developed regarding consciousness. Schleiermacher recognized the gap between the physical and the mental (phenomenal and noumenal) self in Kant's dialectic. He sought to fill this gap by formulating a basis for a whole, embodied self. If this could be accomplished, there would be no need for Kantian dualism. No longer would we 'be' simply because 'we think.' For Schleiermacher, man was more than a spirit within a physical body, greater than a ghost within a machine.

Kant spoke of the 'noumenal self' and the 'phenomenal self,' but never offered a plausible principle of integration for the two.[33] For Thandeka, "Kant characterized human beings as coordinated acts of thinking without acknowledging that this coordinated activity takes place within our organic nature. Kant overlooked the fact that we are beings who think."[34] For

101

Schleiermacher, the principle of 'being' must link both physical and mental capacities. But to demonstrate such a reality would require a tool yet to be appreciated in the philosophic realm. Schleiermacher would find this very apparatus in *Gefühl*.

In the same way that *Gefühl* was a center of faith to Schleiermacher, it was also the grounding principle of man's identity, linking the 'selves' which Kant's philosophy separated. Key to his theory was the delineation of the place from which *Gefühl* emerged. This he would call the *Nullpunkt,* or "nullpoint." He defined it as "that which remains left over" when we are not actually thinking about something.[35] The *Nullpunkt* is the *Indifferenzpunk,* or "point of indifference," at which one organic function has ceased, and the next has yet to begin.[36] For Schleiermacher, this was the common border linking thought with the world around it. And out of this place arises *Gefühl*.

One additional ingredient, however, was necessary in Schleiermacher's defense of his embodied self. He needed a term to denote the objective, metaphysical grounding for thought. This he would name *Anschauung*, or "unmediated intuition."[37] Schleiermacher calls this state 'immediate self-consciousness,' where we are not conscious of 'something,' but we are conscious of 'self.'[38] As Thandeka describes, "This consciousness has no actual content. Rather, our mind is in a state of cessation of thinking." She aptly refers to *Anschauung* as "object-less awareness."[39] A century later American philosopher William James would recognize the existence of this type of state in his masterwork *The Varieties of Religious Experience*:

> "One conclusion was forced upon my mind at that time, and my impression of its truth has ever since remained unshaken. It is that our normal waking consciousness...is but one special type of consciousness, whilst all about it, parted from it by the flimsiest of screens, there lie potential forms of consciousness entirely different."[40]

Schleiermacher was now ready to offer *Gefühl* as the principal link between the noumenal and phenomenal self. For him, *Gefühl* was "the positive expression of the [unity] of our being."[41] If *Nullpunkt* was the location of convergence between physical and mental, and *Anschauung* was the state of immediate self-consciousness, then *Gefühl* was the non-sensate feeling of awareness that emerged out of these. It is through feeling (*Gefühl*) that Schleiermacher links being and thinking. And this is the principal mechanism through which God interacts with man.

In his *On Religion*, Schleiermacher gives a beautiful description of this 'feeling' through which "sense and object mingle and unite." It is worth citing at length as it provides a vivid visualization of complex subject matter:

> "...it is fleeting and transparent as the vapor which the dew breathes on blossom and fruit, it is bashful and tender as a maiden's kiss, it is holy and fruitful as a bridal embrace. Nor is it merely like, it is all this. It is the first contact of the universal life with an individual. It fills no time and fashions nothing palpable. It is the holy wedlock of the Universe with the incarnated Reason for a creative, productive embrace. It is immediate, raised above all error and understanding. You lie directly at the bosom of the infinite world. In that moment, you are its soul. Through one part of your nature you feel, as you own, all its powers and its endless life. In that moment it is your body, you pervade, as your own, its muscles and members and your thinking and forecasting set its inmost nerves in motion. In this way every living, original movement in your life is first received. Among the rest it is the source of every religious emotion. But it is not, as I said, even a moment. The incoming of existence to us, by this immediate union, at once stops as soon as it reaches consciousness. Either the intuition displays itself more vividly and clearly, like the figure of the vanishing mistress to the eyes of her lover; or the feeling issues from your

heart and overspreads your whole being, as the blush of shame and love over the face of a maiden."[42]

In *Gefühl*, Schleiermacher found the unified self that Kant failed to discover. And upon that same principle, he provided philosophy a means to ground *being* fully within organic nature. In other words, man no longer needed to be found 'within the machine.' He could be the whole, unified apparatus. For Schleiermacher, this supplied a way not to deny the metaphysical but to posit a reasonable, naturalistic explanation of it. He would continue to advocate for such a rational faith throughout his career as both a philosopher and theologian.

ADDITIONAL PATHWAYS OF RECONSTRUCTION

In the same way that Friedrich Schleiermacher saved the soul from dualism's separateness, he would go on to reframe much of Christian Orthodoxy, allowing it to be examined in a more reasoned, even naturalistic light. Although Schleiermacher would always consider himself a believer in the supernatural,[43] he rarely found it useful to speak in such terms. He understood the Enlightenment's assumption that there was an inherent conflict between the rational and the supernatural and sought to bring healing to the divide. In defense of his dogmatic work, *The Christian Faith*, Schleiermacher would inquire, "Why is it impossible for persons to be convinced that certain events are supernatural and yet to maintain that they cannot be asked to accept doctrines that are unintelligible and cannot be rationally reconstructed?"[44] It is these doctrines upon which Schleiermacher would take aim as he deemed such reconstruction vital for faith's preservation.

Schleiermacher knew of Hume's critique of miracles and his claim that "firm and unalterable experience" had precluded the belief that natural law could ever be violated. However, Schleiermacher was not convinced that unique acts of the Divine had to be explained by appealing to occurrences outside of the natural realm. To the contrary, he would claim, "It can never be necessary in the interest of religion so to interpret a fact that its dependence on God absolutely excludes its being conditioned upon the system of nature."[45] Schleiermacher was critical of those who assumed God's activity must exist outside nature's domain:

> "Now some have represented miracle...as essential to the perfect manifestation of the divine omnipotence. But it is difficult to conceive, on the one side, how omnipotence is shown to be greater in the suspension of the interdependence of nature than in its original immutable course which was no less divinely ordered. For, indeed, the capacity to make a change in what has been ordained is only a merit in the ordainer, if a change is necessary, which again can only be the result of some imperfection of him or his work."[46]

As a Reformed thinker, Schleiermacher believed God to be omnipotent, decreeing all that has and will ever occur. But even so, he could not countenance a view of the Divine which made it impossible to speak of God in naturalistic terms.

Schleiermacher primarily felt that placing the miraculous in the realm of the supernatural would create problems for the partnership between religion and science. He insisted, "...we should abandon the idea of the absolutely supernatural...In this way everything—even the most wonderful thing that happens or has happened—is a problem for scientific research." And if an event does not lend itself to scientific explanation today, it does not mean that the progress of science would not allow for it to be understood in the future.[47]

The importance Schleiermacher placed on reconsidering inexplicable doctrine would further show in his expositions on beliefs central to the Christian faith, such as the virgin birth. Schleiermacher referred to the virgin birth as "yet another supernatural element." He stated that, "the being of God in Christ cannot possibly be explained by the fact that no male activity had any share in His conception."[48] He felt that the New Testament testimonies of the event were in conflict with the preceding genealogies of Christ and that the original followers of Christ found little value in and made scarce reference to the virgin birth. Schleiermacher posited that Christians who hold to the event's historicity do so because of a perceived need for Jesus not to have part in man's inherited sinful nature, but explained, "where natural procreation was inadequate [to eliminate the passing on of sin], there its partial neutralization must also be inadequate,"[49] since Jesus was still born of Mary. As such, Schleiermacher felt "the assumption of a virgin birth [to be] superfluous." And for those who held to the doctrine, he added the caution, "...it is inadvisable to do so, for this involves one all too easily in investigations of a purely scientific character which lie quite outside our sphere."[50]

Schleiermacher deemed doctrines important that heightened a person's God-consciousness and deepened her 'feeling of absolute dependence on God.' Those dogmas which did not were minimized in value. Schleiermacher would oppose the idea of a supernatural construction of the Bible, a further example, stating:

> "The New Testament canon has obtained its present form through the decision of the church, though this decision cannot be found expressed in any one particular act of declared with exactness. This is not a decision to which we attribute an authority exalted above all inquiry, and thus we are quite justified in starting fresh investigations in connection with earlier waverings on the boundary."[51]

He would even posit the purpose of the Old Testament to exist primarily because of "the appeals the New Testament makes to them." However, because of this, "the Old Testament Scriptures do not on that account share the normative dignity or the inspiration of the New."[52] And even though Schleiermacher would hold the doctrine of the Trinity to be a central tenet of Christianity,[53] he would posit Jesus as someone who was, "...like all men in virtue of the identity of human nature, but distinguished from them all by the contrast potency of His God-consciousness, which was a veritable existence of God in Him."[54]

In Andrew Dole's article, *Schleiermacher and Religious Naturalism*,[55] he claims that "Schleiermacher should be regarded as a religious naturalist in a specific and non-trivial sense of the term."[56] By this, Dole meant that Schleiermacher was committed to a schematic of dogma that positioned religion as a product of the workings of the natural order. Based on the preceding, it is not hard to observe how Dole was able to make this assertion. Indeed, Schleiermacher was instrumental in positioning talk of faith in a rational and sustainable place for the post-Enlightenment era.

GRACE PRIORITIZED

Although Friedrich Schleiermacher became a forerunner to the Christian Naturalists who came after him, he never completely abandoned belief in the supernatural. As referenced above, this was largely due to his deeply es-tablished, Reformed roots. His grandfather, Daniel Schleiermacher, though a reformed preacher, became involved in a radical sect of Millenarians[57] led by Elias Eller. The Ellerian sect was particularly inclined toward mysticism, emotionalism, and radical apocalyptic preaching. It was also a group that fell into scandal and discredit due to accusations of misconduct surrounding Elias and a parishioner.[58] Daniel's father, Gottlieb, witnessed this downfall, which drove him to the arms of orthodoxy and a critical temperament to-wards enthusiastic religious displays.[59] Even though Gottlieb's desire for his son to experience a deeper Christianity was the catalyst for sending Friedrich to live amongst the Moravians, there were elements of conservatism from which he would never be capable of separating.

Chief among these elements was the acclimation towards a determinism in matters of faith. Although this doctrine would take up a relatively small portion of his thousand-page dogmatic work, it was nonetheless present. On matters of soteriology, he would state, "The election of those who are justified is a divine predestination to salvation in Christ."[60] Indeed, for him, we are to consider:

> "...the self-consciousness [Christians] possess as regenerate persons...From the very beginning of our progress in sanctification, it is one with our feeling of absolute dependence, and is bound up with that feeling not only insofar as we are conscious of our activity in the Kingdom of God as an activity *divinely produced* by means of Christ's mission but also in so far as the course of each man's progress is one with the position *assigned him* in the general context of human relationships." (emphasis mine)

For Schleiermacher, the Divine activity undergirds all activity. However, as Stephen Morrison observes in his biographical work, this fact is useful in dispelling the key myth employed to discredit Schleiermacher's dogmatics...that his theology is riddled with subjectivism. In Morrison's words, the standard argument goes as follows:

> "Schleiermacher based his theology on the subjective feelings of human beings, which in turn makes God the highest projection of the human spirit...Schleiermacher speaks of God by speaking of humanity in a loud voice - that is, by projecting the human spirit into the cosmos and calling it 'God.'"[61]

This interpretation is a misreading of Schleiermacher, who posits God as the controlling force behind all creation.[62]

That said, Schleiermacher also offered a unique reframing of the doctrine of election.[63] Whereas for Augustine, Calvin, and Luther, the divine decree was for certain individuals, for Schleiermacher, it was for the election of all humanity:

"We are indeed aware that the preaching of Christ which continually sounds forth from the Church is a living and not unfruitful influence. We see the operations of preparatory grace thus beginning in individuals...we see these individuals going on to become members of the Church."[64]

Indeed, the hope of salvation for Schleiermacher did not end at the point of death but continued posthumously. For those who died as unbelievers, reprobation was still an 'intermediate state:'[65]

"Suppose an individual in whom noteworthy influences of preparatory grace are to be seen, but about whom it may be equally certain that he is not yet in the state of sanctification...we proceed on the definite assumption that all belonging to the human race are eventually taken up into living fellowship with Christ...the state in which he dies is only an intermediate state."

It is hard to read Schleiermacher without noting the sense of love and grace with which he adorned his voluminous writings and preaching.[66]

And just as, for him, election was a decree for the whole of humanity (not simply the individual), so was his conception of a life well-lived a call for life in community. For him, the Church community was a centerpiece of his practical theology, comprising large sections of his dogmatics as well as his work in Christian ethics. For him, ethics, "could not have found its foundation anywhere else but in the doctrine of the Christian church."[67]

Schleiermacher scholar Terrence Tice notes that what was true in Schleiermacher's words also exemplified his deeds. Though known primarily for his extensive works in theology, philosophy, hermeneutics,[68] and ethics, Schleiermacher was always involved directly in ministry. He was involved in most aspects of pastoral service and many levels of church government.[69] In his personal life, Schleiermacher constantly surrounded himself with loved ones. As Tice notes:

> "It was a warm, busy household, the marriage was loving and sound, and he was much engaged with his large family. For additional companionship, Schleiermacher enjoyed numerous friends and colleagues in his 'outside, public' life. Frequently, he had a friend or students 'in' for lunch of tea. There were family trips to...distant places...concerts and various public events."

Schleiermacher's passion for people and ministry would remain through his last days. In 1834, ten days before his passing, we find Schleiermacher regretful that he does not have more time to continue his important work. As family and friends urged him to rest and resign from his many positions of influence, he responded:

> "Shall I take my rest? It is what I cannot do. My lectures are of too much importance with me to be discontinued; more important still is the religious instruction of the youth; and most of all the preaching of the gospel."[70]

Days later, Schleiermacher would pass. But, while the man was no longer among us, the legacy would remain. Father of Modern Theology is an apt title for the person who made such a difference in the way faith is approached. He recentered religion, giving primacy to the experience of God, and making secondary all reason, tradition, and dogma. He took on the challenges of Enlightenment deconstruction and, in doing so, reconstructed what it meant to be in a relationship with the Divine. Though few outside of the academic world of theology know his name, all who call themselves Christian owe him an unspeakable debt, for he shaped our approach to faith itself.

It is appropriate here to let one of Schleiermacher's fiercest critics have the last word, since even he cannot avoid paying homage to the man who helped to craft our theological culture:

"Schleiermacher merits detailed historical consideration and study even if only because he was the one in whom the great struggle of Christianity with the strivings and achievements of the German spirit in 1750-1830, in whose light or shadow we still stand today, took place in a way which would still be memorable even if he were dead and his theological work had been transcended...But Schleiermacher is not dead for us and his theological work has not been transcended. If anyone still speaks today in Protestant theology as though he were still among us, it is Schleiermacher. We *study* Paul and the reformers, but we *see* with the eyes of Schleiermacher and think along the same lines he did."[71]

THE MONOLOGEN

The collection of Friedrich Schleiermacher's writing comprises well over forty volumes of work. His anthology includes numerous essays covering various topics, decades of sermons, years of class lectures, the translation of Plato's body of work into German, translations of Aristotle, writings on hermeneutics, Christian ethics, philosophy, dogmatics, and much more. Among this myriad of materials, three works stand out as particularly significant: *The Christian Faith, On Religion: Speeches to its Cultured Despisers*, and *The Monologen.*

The Christian Faith stands clearly as Schleiermacher's masterwork. First published in 1821, it is Schleiermacher's thousand-page comprehensive dogmatic tome and is considered to be one of the most important volumes of theology ever written. It carefully correlates the whole of Christian doctrine with its impact on human experience and 'God-consciousness,' and is the basis for the apt title Schleiermacher has since received as Father of Modern Theology.

On Religion, Speeches to its Cultured Despisers was Schleiermacher's first notable work. Published in 1799, it contained the young theologian's apologetic response to those Enlightenment thinkers who attempted to deconstruct religion, replacing it solely with reason and the fruits of scientific progress. It is comprised of five speeches. The first served to defend religion as a pathway beyond the consciousness of self to that of the "Eternal and Holy."[72] In his second (most famous) speech, Schleiermacher outlined the nature of religion as neither "modes of knowing or modes of acting," but, "to feel...that our being and living is being and living in and through God."[73] In speech three, Schleiermacher spoke to the cultivation of religion within humanity. The fourth speech is a discourse on the social elements of religion, namely the church and the priesthood. In speech five, Schleiermacher addressed the plurality of religious views within the Church and among the various non-Christian religions.

After the positive reception of Schleiermacher's *Speeches*, Schleiermacher grew in both public esteem and self-confidence. Shortly after its publication, he would write his sister to express his new-found enthusiasm:

> "I wish you could share the quiet joy which possesses my soul. I rejoice over the past, and for the present, and I look with equanimity toward the future, whatever it may bring. I can say with reasonable certainty that this will be my ruling mood as long as I live, for it is grounded in my inmost self."[74]

It is in the wake of the success of *On Religion*, that Schleiermacher penned what was to become known as his 'spiritual autobiography,'[75] *The Monologen*.

Written in the span of only four weeks, Schleiermacher followed up his five speeches with five monologues (or soliloquies), through which he would paint an intimate depiction of his inmost spiritual life. It would quickly supplement his popular apologetic with a portrait of a man caught between the worlds of Enlightenment and Romanticism.

The five soliloquies found in the Monologen are titled *Reflection, Soundings, The World, Prospect,* and *Youth and Age. Reflection* is an elucidation of meditation. It examines differing modes of introspection employed, as each person takes account of her own life. Schleiermacher considers how many focus on the "happy imagery" of the "outer world," but never "penetrate beneath the surface."[76] Along with an overemphasis on temporary existence comes "its irresistible decline from sunny heights into a dread night of annihilation." He insists not to "mistake the atmosphere for the world around which it has formed." For, "Whoever sees and recognizes only the outward spectacle of life...will always remain a slave of Time and Necessity."[77]

Schleiermacher, instead, suggests looking inward, realizing:

> "When I withdraw into myself...my eyes are lifted from the realm of time, and my vision free from every restriction of Necessity. Every oppressive feeling of bondage disappears, my spirit discovers its creative nature, the light of God begins to shine upon me, banishing far hence the mists in which enslaved humanity strays in error."[78]

In closing, he famously admonished, "Be not troubled for the future, nor weep for things which pass, but take heed lest you lose yourself, and weep if you are swept along the stream of time, without carrying heaven with you."[79]

Monologue two, *Soundings,* is written as Schleiermacher's spiritual awakening. In it, the one who sees the external is juxtaposed against the person who views life from an inward perspective. "But oh, the shame of it, that anyone should see himself only as one stranger sees another!"[80] Schleiermacher describes his awakening, recalling:

"With proud joy, I still recall the time, when I discovered humanity and knew that henceforth I should never lose it. The sublime revelation came from within; it was not produced by any code of ethics or system of philosophy."[81]

Here, Schleiermacher contrasts his discovery with that of Kant's Categorical Imperative. "Neither do I strive since then to acquire this or that particular virtue...as are those whose fleeting existence is only now and then visited by a dubious gleam of innate reason."[82] Schleiermacher admits, "For a long time I too was content with the discovery of universal reason." But he eventually, "...saw clearly that each man is meant to represent humanity in his own way."[83]

He adds that the life which peers inward can only subsist in the presence of love. "Without love, the very first attempt at self-formation would prove shattering because of the frightful disproportion between giving and receiving." Schleiermacher encapsulates the essence of this soliloquy by saying:

"Love, thou force of gravitation in the spiritual world, no individual life and no development is possible without thee...though art alpha and omega. No development without love, and without individual development no perfection in love; each supplements the other, both increase indivisibly."[84]

He ends *Soundings* by devoting extended time to the concept of friendship, after which he proclaims, "But then, in such a perfect love the individuals themselves are also made perfect."

Monologue three is entitled *The World*. Like *Soundings*, it is a contrast between life lived through an 'outward' perspective and one lived with a spiritual lens. However, this time, the focus is on life in community. For Schleiermacher, there are those whose view of the world is one of collective resignation. These people, "neither vainly grieve nor falsely hope." Such contentment, he laments, "...is but folly's passage from hope in life to contempt for it...the hollow echo of footsteps reluctantly moving on from youth to age."[85]

Schleiermacher suggests that his demands "are not so modest as to be content with the improvement of man's relation to external nature."[86] Instead, he proposes a "higher, more intimate, spiritual community."[87] This community is simply a multiplicity of like-minded, inward-looking people. It can be made of spouses, friends, or citizens of the same country. The objective is "extending to each other the hand of fellowship," with the result being, "something greater than each could achieve independently."[88] Indeed, when we, "exchange knowledge, show sympathy, [and] mitigate sufferings," we achieve what is highest in life.

We are to be a light of hope for humanity and expect others to be the same for us. Schleiermacher rejoices when he observes this happening. As he so eloquently puts it:

"But wherever I do see a spark of the hidden fire that must sooner or later consume the outworn and recreate the world, I am drawn to it with love and true hope as a welcome sign of my distant home."[89]

As we journey from *inner reflection* (monologue one) to *spiritual awakening* (monologue two), to the formation of a *spiritual community* (monologue three), we are brought to monologue four, which Schleiermacher names *Prospect*. This soliloquy deals with the issue of *destiny*. He opens by asking, "Is it true that we all walk the earth under the dispensation of powers not our own, and live uncertain of the future?" For, if this is the case, man must simply be "the toy of chance." He states that the only way to avoid these implications is to not be "preoccupied with the insecure possession of external things."[90] He encourages the reader to instead lay hold of their true (inner) self. Only then will we live in freedom. We will be the master of the future instead of the future being ours.

So then, what may the purpose of external circumstances be? For Schleiermacher, they are an opportunity. Changing circumstances "express the nature of [one's] being and afford [her] new material for its inner growth and cultivation."[91] Indeed, we must never fear losing such freedom for, "A man must sell himself in order to become a slave, and fate dares bid only for one who offers himself at a price."[92]

Prospect expresses Schleiermacher's constant desire to achieve higher worlds of existence by adding to his life the fellowship that comes with marriage and deep friendships. But he states that no external extravagances will circumvent his inner development. For he may realize these things still, if only in "the divine power of imagination."[93]

Schleiermacher closes by confessing his outer circumstances will never truly reflect the beauty of his inner life. For him, this will be a continual quest. For it is only in this perfection that he will be ready to die. And he will "approach [this] end from all sides."[94]

The *Monologen's* fifth and final soliloquy is entitled *Youth and Age*. It is as apt an ending to a spiritual autobiography as can be desired since it contains Schleiermacher's chief ingredient for achieving his personal goals: *perspective*. Here, Schleiermacher contrasts 'age' as a paradigm measured in time with 'age' as a measure of spiritual maturity. He opens by opining, "Were I now convinced that youth would escape me with the flight of years, I should voluntarily hasten to meet an early death, lest fear of certain misery to come embitter every good of the present."[95] But for the young romanticist, youth has nothing to do with the amount of decay one's physical body has experienced. Rather, it is a state of mind. "Be not a fool, to prophecy the spirit's strength in terms of time, for time can never be its measure!"[96] Indeed, "Old age is but an idle prejudice, an ugly fruit of a mad delusion that the spirit is dependent on the body."[97]

Physical age does not impede the spiritually minded. Even in advanced years, one can maintain the same, if not greater, strength of spirit. It is this hope that Schleiermacher vows to carry with him all his days. And there is freedom in such a hope. Our happiness, our wonder, our sense and taste for adventure should never be quelled by Time's passage. Schleiermacher closes his Monologen with these words. Words that we will do well to not only heed but embrace with our inmost being:

> "Shun frugal behavior! Let life be unconfined; no power is ever lost, unless you repress it within yourself, and leave it unused. Let not your will for today be determined by your wish for tomorrow... [It is] a stupid self-deception to think that you want what you do not want! Let not the world tell you how to serve it and when...attempt nothing unless it proceeds freely from a love and desire within your soul. And let no limit be set upon your love, no measure of kind or of duration!"[98]

SCHLEIERMACHER'S SOLILOQUIES

THE MONOLOGEN

Preface to the Second Edition

Dr. Fr. Schleiermacher,
Berlin, April, 1810

WHEN THIS LITTLE BOOK went out of print, I did not wish to refuse the publication of a second edition. In part, because I am indebted to the book for attracting readers of generous spirit in a way I had hardly expected, and for bringing me highly esteemed friends. And then also because such a refusal to reprint might be misinterpreted as a recantation. Let me, therefore, render thanks to these pages by granting them a new lease of life, at the same time explaining that all the sentiments expressed in them are still my own as fully as any portrait drawn in early life can and should resemble one's older self. But in reediting the book I must confess that the difficulties involved in touching up a work like this, to say nothing of revising it, are all too great, because there is danger, on the one hand, of clouding its essential, inner truth by an unconscious infusion of characteristics of a later period, or on the other hand, of disturbing friendly readers by changes which might appear arbitrary. For these reasons I prefer to republish it with all its imperfections, and except in small matters of expression I have made only a few changes noted down soon after its first appearance, because they seemed to clarify some obscurities and to prevent misunderstandings. Therefore, if anyone finds fault with the manner in which the book is written rather than with its content, let him not attribute the defect to me as I am now, but rather to the man I was when this book first appeared. But if there be others who find the very spirit of the book uncongenial, and who are unwilling or unable to distinguish between a man's ideal self and his mere appearance, nothing need hinder them from serving up again the flat and tasteless ridicule heard here and there ten years ago.

Preface to the Third Edition
S., Berlin, December, 1821

IN PUBLISHING THIS THIRD edition of my little book I refer the reader again to the justification given in the preface to the second edition, and shall attempt only a few additional words for the benefit of those who may have really misinterpreted what the book aims to accomplish. Since the second edition was published, an intimate friend of long acquaintance made the following very pertinent statement. The life of every individual, as it appears to others, suggests at one time his essential, archetypal self, and at another his distorted self. Now only when following out the first suggestion, that toward the archetypal self, can self-examination yield results fit for publication and communicable to others; introspection in the other direction, toward the distorted self, is soon lost too deep in those recesses of the private life which, as some sage has already said, a man had best conceal even from himself. He who passes over this latter type of introspection, as was attempted in this book, while communicating his findings in the former, obviously with the special intention of locating the points of difference between archetypal selves, is completely misinterpreted if he is censured for seeing himself only in a favorable light, and for being more ridiculous than Narcissus, in that he goes so far as to publish for the whole wide world to read the language of infatuation which he has addressed to his own likeness. Moreover, to this purpose of the book can be attributed the fact that self-examination assumes in it a purely ethical form, and that what is in a narrow sense religious should nowhere be prominent therein. But I did not intend this to favor the view that religious introspection must tend only in the opposite direction of contemplating man's distorted, fallen self. On the contrary, it has long been my plan to refute this one-sided conception also, and to supplement this book by a similar series of religious meditations. But thus far time has not permitted me to do so.

Offering

NO CHOICER GIFT CAN any man give to another than his spirit's intimate converse with itself. For this affords the highest boon there is, a clear and undistorted insight into a free being. No gift is more enduring, for nothing can destroy the satisfaction, which such an insight has once granted you, and its intrinsic truth assures your love so that you delight in beholding it again. None is surer proof against the lust and guile of others, since it arouses no desire that is not spiritual, and offers no secondary attractions that could lead to its abuse. If anyone stands aloof, and looks askance at this precious treasure, attributing to it absurd features which your honest eye does not detect, let not such idle mockery rob you of your joy. Heed it as little as I shall let myself repent of having shared with you that which I had to give. Come, take the gift, ye who can understand my spirit's thought! May my feelings here intoned be an accompaniment to the melody within yourselves, and may the shock which passes through you at the contact with my spirit, become a quickening impulse in your life.

Reflection

THE OUTER WORLD IN its eternal laws as well as in its most ephemeral appearances, like a magic mirror, doubtless reflects our highest and innermost nature in a thousand tender and sublime similitudes. But this happy imagery, the delicate charm of which should enliven and inform dull sensibilities as it plays upon them, is of no avail to such as disregard the plain demands of their own deepest feelings and do not hear the subdued sighing of their abused spirit. The true significance and inner purport of outward relations escapes them, even of such as their own genius has contrived and must repeatedly bring to light. Thus (in the reckoning of the calendar), we divide the infinite line of time into equal portions, at points determined arbitrarily by the most trivial circumstances, having no significance in our lives and determining nothing, since nought proceeds at an exact pace, not the structure of our work, nor the round of our emotions, nor the play of our destiny. And yet these arbitrary divisions are meant to be something more than an aid to the chronologer or a feast for the mathematician; to everyone they must inevitably suggest serious reflections on the possibility of dividing life. But few are they who penetrate beneath the surface of this profound allegory, and understand to what truth this very natural suggestion points.

The average individual recognizes nothing but his transient existence, and its irresistible decline from sunny heights into a dread night of annihilation. He thinks some hidden hand draws the thread of his life along, alternately weaving and unweaving a web of sensations and ideas, pulling it together now loosely, now tightly, and that nothing more exists. The swifter the succession of our thoughts and feelings, the richer their variety, the more harmonious and intimate their combination, the more glorious and perfect a work of art our life is believed to be. And could men also explain in mechanistic fashion the entire nexus of such a life, they would regard themselves as having reached the summit of humanity and of self-comprehension. But in thinking thus they mistake the reflected image of their activity for the whole activity itself, those outer contact-points, wherein the energies of the self meet with external things, for their inmost being, they mistake the atmosphere for the world about which it has formed. How could such men, (watching the old year out and awaiting the new), with reflections no deeper than these, understand the challenge implicit in this very act of dividing time? The point which cuts a line is not part of that line; it is related to the Infinite as truly and more immediately than to the line, and anywhere along the line you can place such a point. Just so, the moment in which you cut the course of life and make a new division, should be no portion of your temporal existence; you should regard it otherwise, and in it become conscious of your immediate relations to the Infinite and Eternal; and whenever you will, such a moment can be yours. Seeing herein a sublime intimation of the Divine in me, I rejoice in its invitation to an immortal life outside the realm of time and free from its harsh laws! But those, who do not recognize a call to this higher life, while immersed in transient thought and feeling, will equally fail to apprehend it when, without really knowing what they are about, they resort to the measurement of time for the sake of marking off periods in their mundane existence. Better that they never even suspected the truth than that their vain energetic bustle should so painfully disconcert me when I strive to obey the divine invitation! Doubtless they too demand a point in time, which shall mean more than a merely transient present, but they have not the wit to apprehend it as Eternity. Often for a moment, sometimes perhaps for an hour or even for a day, they will actually absolve themselves from the obligations of assiduous industry, from the eager quest for knowledge and pleasure, warned as they needs must be of the transiency of their interests, by the reflection that the present is ever slipping into the past as speedily as it emerges out of the future. There follows disillusionment and disgust with all this useless pursuit of novel enjoyments, perceptions, or activities; they sit down on the bank of the river of life, and with a helpless smile let fall their tears into the dancing waves below. Like barbarous savages who kill the wives, the children, or the slaves beside a father's grave, so at the close of a departing year they sacrifice the holiday, dissipating it in empty imaginings, a thoroughly vain oblation.

Meditation and contemplation are without profit for him who does not know the inner life of spirit. Let him not struggle to escape from temporal things, who recognizes nothing timeless in himself. For whither should he mount from the stream of time, and what could he win save useless suffering and a feeling of annihilation? One man balances the joys and sorrows of the past, seeking to focus upon a single image, under the lens of memory, the faint light that still glimmers out of the distance which he has traversed. Another reviews his achievements; it pleases him to recall his arduous struggle against the world and fate; and happy that matters have not turned out worse, he notes here and there some monument to his effort, fashioned out of the stuff of a reality indifferent to his aims, though, of course, it falls far short of his intentions. Still a third takes stock of his learning, and struts with pride because of his much increased and well-appointed store of knowledge, delighted in his power to contain it all. What puerile attempts of an idle conceit are these! The first no longer thinks of the cares which his imagination raised for him, and which his memory blushes to preserve; the second turns his back upon the world and fate, refusing altogether to acknowledge the support they gave him; the third does not take into account the old knowledge that was crowded out by the new, the thoughts that thinking excluded, and the impressions that were sacrificed to learning. Thus the reckoning is never right. And if it were, how deeply pained I am to think that men can imagine this to be self-contemplation or call this knowledge of oneself! How miserably their much-glorified business of self-examination ends! Imagination fixes on a faithful portrait of the past, projects it with lavish embellishments upon the empty canvass of the immediate future, and yet looks back with many a sigh toward the original. The ultimate gain of such introspection reduces itself to the idle hope of a better future, and the vain lament that bygone pleasures are no more, and that life's substance as it wanes from day to day gives warning that its bright flame will soon expire. With such idle wishes and vain complaints Time grievously brands her slaves who would escape; the best are like unto the worst for she will just as surely overtake the best eventually. Whoever sees and recognizes only the outward spectacle of life instead of the spiritual activity that secretly stirs his inmost being, who merely constructs a picture of life and its vicissitudes from impressions gathered far and near instead of facing his essential self, will always remain a slave of Time and Necessity. All his thoughts and feelings bear their stamp, are still in their possession, and he may never set foot within the sacred precincts of Freedom, even though he thinks he has attained self-consciousness. For in the image which he constructs of himself, this very self becomes something external, like all else, and everything in such an image is determined by external circumstances. What he sees in it, the thoughts and feelings that it arouses, depend alike on the content of the moment and on his particular condition of life. If he has looked for nought but the gratification of animal sense, he will judge life rich or poor according to the number of agreeable moments it contains, and the immediate satisfaction which he takes in such a retrospect will depend on whether the greatest pleasures! came first or last. If he wanted to create and to enjoy beauty, he will court the judgment passed upon him, and is dependent furthermore upon the conditions and materials that fate has provided for his work. In like dependence is he who sought to signalize his life with benefactions. They all must bow beneath the scepter of Necessity, and bear the curse of transiency, which permits nothing to endure.

Their sense of life is like my mood when some artfully constructed harmony of many notes has struck my ear but is now silent; the imagination plagues itself with a meagre echo, and the soul yearns for that which will not return. Life indeed is but a fleeting harmony rising from the contact of the temporal and the eternal, but man is a permanent creation, an undying object of contemplation. Only his innermost activity, wherein his true nature abides, is free, and in contemplating it, I feel myself to be upon the holy ground of Freedom, far from every debasing limitation. I must fix my eyes upon my true self, if each moment is not to slip away as merely so much time, instead of being grasped as an element of Eternity, and transmuted into a higher and freer life.

He alone enjoys freedom and eternity who knows what man is and what the world is who has reached clarity in solving the great enigma of their differentiation and their interaction, a riddle in whose dark and ancient mazes thousands still are caught, and needs must follow servilely the most deceptive illusions, because their own light has failed them. What the multitude calls the world, I call man, and what they call man, I call the world. To them the world is ever primary, and the spirit but a humble guest upon it, uncertain of his place and powers. To me the spirit is the first and only being for what I take to be the world, is the fairest creation of spirit, a mirror in which it is reflected. In awe and fear the multitude cower before the infinitely vast and ponderous masses of the material world, amid which man appears so small and insignificant. To me all this is but the giant body common to Humanity, belonging to us even as an individual's body does to him, made possible through Humanity alone, to which it is given in order that the human spirit may master it and be revealed therein. The creative freedom of Humanity is exercised upon this body, to sense all its pulsations, to mold and transmute all its features into organs of human life, and to delineate all its parts with the spirit's regal presence. Is there indeed a body without a spirit? Does not the body exist only because and insofar as the spirit requires it and is conscious thereof? All those feelings that seem to be forced upon me by the material world are in reality my own free doing; nothing is a mere effect of that world upon me, every real influence is exerted by me upon it; that world is not, in fact, distinct from me, nor antithetic to me. For this very reason I do not choose to dignify it with the name of world, a great word implying omnipresence and omnipotence. The only reality that I deem worthy to be called a world is the eternal community of spiritual beings, their influence upon each other, their mutual development, the sublime harmony of freedom. This infinite totality of spiritual beings is the only reality that I recognize over against my finite and individual self. This reality alone I suffer to transform and shape the surface of my being; this heaven alone shall mold me. Here, and here only is the province of necessity. My activity itself is free, not so my function in the world, for that obeys eternal laws. Freedom finds its limit in another freedom, and whatever happens freely bears marks of limitation and community. Yes, holy Freedom, in all reality thou art first! It is thou that dwellest within me and in everyone. Outside us is Necessity, a chord determined by the harmonious clash of various inner liberties that thus reveal themselves. Within me I can behold nought but Freedom, necessity reigns not in my doing, but in the reflection thereof, in the perceptions I have of the world which I help to create in holy association with all other beings. To this realm of necessity belongs whatever I have produced in working on a common foundation with others; such productions are my share in the joint creation that expresses our inner thought. To necessity belong also the rising and falling tides of emotion, the train of images that passes before us, and everything that changes in our souls with time. Such images and feelings are a token that the spirit and the world have met in harmony, ever renewing the kiss of friendship between them in a different manner. The Dance of Hours thus proceeds, melodious and harmonious, according to a necessary rhythm. But Freedom plays the melody, selects the key, and all the subtle modulations are her work. For these proceed from an inner determination and from the individual's unique disposition.

And so, Freedom, you are for me the soul and principle of all things. When I withdraw into myself to contemplate you, my eyes are lifted from the realm of time, and my vision free from every restriction of Necessity. Every oppressive feeling of bondage disappears, my spirit discovers its creative nature, the light of God begins to shine upon me, banishing far hence the mists in which enslaved humanity strays in error. The self-revealed in my meditations is no longer a creature of fate or fortune; the hours of happiness I have deserved, the results achieved by my efforts, and whatever I have actually put into execution, all these are of the world; they are not myself. If my activity is designed to bring humanity into possession of its massive body, the material world, giving this body life and organic fitness, or by artful imitation fashioning it in the image of reason and mind, the extent to which I find the earth already suited to my purpose, the ease with which its crude mass can be molded and brought under the control of spirit, is but a sign of the dominion which Freedom has already exercised over it in the person of others. It indicates what still remains to be done, but furnishes no measure of what I do. My view of my conduct and picture of my whole being is unchanged; I am no better or no worse in my own eyes, whether external circumstances are propitious or unfavorable to my activity. I do not discover in myself the slave, for whom the world or ironbound necessity decides what he may become. And just as pain does not easily deprive a strong and healthy soul of control over the physical body, so too I sense my free dominion over the material world, regardless of whether the consequences be pleasurable or painful. The inner life reveals itself alike in either case, and its creation is an act of spiritual freedom. If the purpose of my actions is to shape what is human in me, giving it a particular form and definite characteristics, thus contributing to the world by my own self-development and offering to the community of free spiritual beings the unique expression of my own freedom, then I see no difference whether or not my efforts are at once combined with those of others and some objective result immediately appears to greet me as part of the world-order. My efforts have not been vain, if only I myself acquire greater individuality and independence, for through such self-development I also contribute to the world, no matter how soon or late the actions of others combine with my own to produce some new, visible result. Unlike those who have not discovered the inner life, and who think to find themselves in particulars of the outward life, I am never depressed by self-contemplation, nor need I ever lament a broken will or a defeated purpose.

Having clearly differentiated between the inner and the outer, I know who I am, and I find myself only in the inner life, in external things I see only the world. My spirit knows how to distinguish both, and does not fluctuate between the two, as is common, in unenlightened confusion. Hence, I also know where Freedom is to be sought and the sacred sense of its presence, that ever refuses to bless him whose vision rests solely upon the outward life and work of man. However deeply such a one may involve himself in end-less mazes of speculation, turning the problem over and over, and however effective he may be in action, the conception of Freedom is beyond the reach of his thought. He follows not only the actual indications of necessity, but in slavish and superstitious submission to his false philosophy he must look for them and believe them to be present, even where he does not see them.

Freedom seems to him nothing but an illusion, spread like a veil over a hidden and uncomprehended necessity. Moreover, such an empiricist, whose action and whose thought look outward, sees everything as finite and particular. He cannot imagine himself as other than a sum of fleeting appearances, each of which supplants and cancels the other, so that it is impossible to conceive them as a whole. A complete picture of his being thus eludes him in a thousand contradictions. Indeed, in the realm of outward behavior particulars are often contradictory; action destroys passivity, thought supplants sensation, and contemplation forces the will to be at rest. But within the spirit all is one, each action is but supplementary to another, in each the other also is preserved. Thus self-contemplation lifts me far above the finite, which may be seen entire as a determined series with definite limits. No action transpires within me, that I can truly regard as isolated, and none of which I could say that it constitutes a whole by itself. Each of my acts reveals the whole of my being, undivided, each of its manifestations goes with the rest; there are no limits at which introspection can halt, it must ever remain unfinished, if it is to remain true to life. Nor can I divine my own being in its entirety without contemplating Humanity, and determining my rank and place in its domain. And who can think of Humanity without being lost in thought of the pure spirit's infinite realm and nature?

It is this higher order of self-contemplation, and this alone that makes me capable of meeting the sublime summons that man live not only as a mortal in the realm of time, but also as immortal in the domain of eternity, that his life be not only earthly but also divine. The stream of time bears with it in its course my mortal deeds; ideas and feelings change, I cannot hold fast a single one. The scene of life, as I picture it, hurries by; upon the next inevitable wave the stream will carry me on toward something new. But as often as I turn my gaze inward upon my inmost self, I am at once within the domain of eternity. I behold the spirit's action, which no world can change, and no time can destroy, but which itself creates both world and time. Nor do I require the challenge of that special hour, in which one year gives way to another, to arouse me to this appreciation of the eternal, and to open the eyes of the spirit, closed perhaps in slumber though the heart beats and the limbs are active. Who once has tasted it will want to lead the divine life continually; every act should be accompanied by an insight into spiritual mysteries, and in every moment man can dwell beyond the moment, in the higher world.

Of course, wise men say: to live is one thing, and to lose oneself in the ultimate sources and highest reaches of thought is another. Content yourself modestly with one of them, for while the passage of time keeps you busy with the affairs of the world, you cannot also contemplate the inmost depths of your being without distraction. Artists say that, when you are creating a picture or composing a poem, the mind must lose itself completely in its work, and must not reflect upon its own behavior. Nevertheless, dare to try, my soul, in spite of these reasonable warnings! Press forward toward your own goal, which may be different from that of artists and sages. Man can do more than he supposes; yet even when he strives toward the highest, he can but achieve in part. If a sage's thought, even in its most intimate and profound reaches, can be an external force of influence and guidance in the world, then why should not an outward act, of whatever nature, at the same time imply its own inward consideration? If the divine source of all art and poetry is spiritual introspection, and if the spirit finds within its own being all that it can express in its immortal creations, why should not every creative act of artist or poet, being but the expression of what is within him involve self-contemplation? Divide not your being, my soul, it is a permanent whole that cannot forego its activity nor the knowledge thereof without self-destruction! Let your influence be everywhere felt, and accomplish all that you can; follow the lead of your natural limitations and cultivate every means of spiritual association; bring out what is individual in you, and place the impress of your spirit on all that is about you; collaborate in the consecrated tasks of mankind, attracting to yourself such spirits as are congenial. But throughout all be ever mindful of your inner self, know what you are about, and in what character you are acting. The idea, by which men imagine they have intellectually grasped the Deity, a thing they never can do, has at least the truth of a poetic symbol of what humanity should be. The spirit sustains its world by the mere fact of its being, and the eternal, unchanging activity which produces its diverse acts issues from its own free will. Itself unmoved, it contemplates its own activity, ever new and ever yet the same; this contemplation is immortality and eternal life, for therein the spirit requires nothing but itself, and contemplation never lacks its object, nor does the object lack the contemplating mind. In such terms men have also tried to imagine immortality, but all too content with the earthly life they aspire to it only after death. Their mythology is more profound than they. In truth, to the sensuous mind an inner process can seem but the shadow of an outward act, and in such a realm of shadows men have placed the soul forever, lamenting that the grey existence there below affords them but a meagre suggestion of their present life. But this spiritual life, which scant imagination exiles into subterranean darkness, is truly of Olympian clarity, and the realm of shadows may serve me here on earth as archetype of reality. God is thought to be outside the world of time, and after death man is to be freed forever from temporal limitations in order to behold and praise the Deity. But even now the spirit spans the world of time, Eternity is in the sight thereof, and the celestial rapture of immortal choirs. Wherefore begin at once your life eternal in the constant contemplation of your own true being. Be not troubled for the future, nor weep for things which pass, but take heed lest you lose yourself, and weep if you are swept along in the stream of time, without carrying heaven within you.

Soundings

MANKIND IS SHY OF self-analysis, and many people tremble slavishly when they can no longer dodge the question of what they have done, what they have become, and who they really are. The thing frightens them; they know not what will come of it. It seems to them easier for a man to judge another person than himself, and after strict self-scrutiny they rather claim the grace of modesty in giving themselves the benefit of the doubt. And yet it is only willfulness that hides a person from himself; his judgment cannot err provided he really faces himself. But it is just this which people neither can nor want to do. The spell of life and of the world is upon them, and resolved not to turn from that spectacle, all that they discover of themselves is but a vague and delusive reflection. To be sure, I can judge another person only by his acts, for I never look upon his inner disposition. I can never know at first-hand what his purpose actually was; I simply compare his deeds with one another, and from these I make a precarious inference as to his aims and the spirit which moved him. But oh, the shame of it, that anyone should see himself only as one stranger sees another that anyone should remain ignorant of his inner life and even plume himself on his supposed shrewdness, if he succeeds in grasping the last link of a chain of resolutions that issued in overt action, together with the feeling that attended it and the idea that immediately preceded it! How can such a one ever know either himself or others? What is to guide him in conjecturing inner realities from external facts, if he does not base his judgment on a crucial experience of something immediately certain? The inevitable presentiment of error makes him afraid, the overshadowing suspicion that he is culpable in his error oppresses his heart, and his thoughts vacillate in terror of that little portion of self-consciousness which men still carry with them, generally degraded to the role of a harsh disciplinarian, whose voice they needs must often hear unwillingly.

In truth, men have good cause for anxiety, lest in honestly probing the inner motives of their lives, they fail to recognize what is truly human there, and see the conscience, which is consciousness of true humanity, sadly mutilated. For whoever has not scrutinized his previous conduct can give no security that in the future he will remember that he is a human being or prove himself worthy of the name. If he has once broken the thread of self-consciousness, if he has but once abandoned himself to those feelings and impressions that he shares with brutes, how can he know whether he has not fallen into sheer brutality? To behold humanity within oneself, and never to lose sight of the vision when once found, is the only certain means of never straying from its sacred precincts. This vision is the intimate and necessary tie between conduct and the perception of truth, a connection mysterious and unintelligible only to fools and men of dull sensibility. A truly human way of acting produces a clear consciousness of what is essentially human, and this in turn permits of no other behavior than such as is worthy of humanity. He who can never lift himself to this clear insight is ever the sport of vague instinctive premonitions; in vain you will undertake to educate and train him. For all his ingenuity and for all his bold resolution to force his way back into the circle of humanity, the sacred portals will not open. He remains outside on profane ground, and he will not escape the pursuit of the offended godhead, nor the shameful feeling that he is an exile from his true fatherland. It is sheer folly and vain trifling to make experiments or to lay down rules in the realm of freedom. To be a man calls for a single free resolve; he who has taken that resolve will always remain one; he who ceases to be one has never taken it.

With proud joy I still recall the time when I discovered humanity and knew that henceforth I should never lose it. The sublime revelation came from within; it was not produced by any code of ethics or system of philosophy. My long quest which neither this nor that would satisfy was crowned in one moment of insight; freedom dissolved my dark doubts by a single act.

I can affirm that since then I have never forsaken my true self. I no longer know the thing that men call conscience; no qualm now reproves me, and I need none to warn me. Neither do I strive since then to acquire this or that particular virtue, nor am I especially elated by some particular act, as are those whose fleeting existence is only now and then visited by a dubious gleam of innate reason. In quiet tranquility, in utter simplicity I preserve within me an uninterrupted consciousness of humanity's entire essence. With pleasure and confidence, I often survey my behavior in all its bearings, being assured that I shall find nothing which humanity must needs repudiate. If this were all that I exacted of myself, I might long since have found inward peace, and awaited the end of my existence with perfect composure! For the certainty I have attained is unshakeable, and I should deem it a culpable piece of cowardice, such as is foreign to my nature, were I to look to a long life for fuller confirmation of my inner conviction, fearing that after all, something might yet happen that could plunge me from the height of reason into an abyss of sheer brutishness. And yet, I too am still troubled with doubts. For when I had reached my first goal, another and a higher appeared before me, and since it appears sometimes clearly and then again dimly, self-scrutiny does not always tell me by what path I can approach it, or where I stand with reference to it. On these points my judgment wavers. But it is confirmed and gains conviction the more often I return to examine myself. And however far I were from certainty, I should still search in silence and without complaint, for stronger than my doubt is my great joy in having found out what I should seek, and in escaping from the great illusion which deceives many of the best throughout their lives and keeps them from soaring to the true summits of humanity. For a long time, I too was content with the discovery of a universal reason; I worshipped the one essential being as the highest, and so believed that there is but a single right way of acting in every situation, that the conduct of all men should be alike, each differing from the other only by reason of his place and station in the world. I thought humanity revealed itself as varied only in the manifold diversity of outward acts, that man himself, the individual, was not a being uniquely fashioned, but of one substance and everywhere the same.

Thus is it ever with mankind! When, turning with discontent from the unworthy particularity of a sensuous animal life, man wins a realization of humanity in its universal aspects and submits himself to duty, he is not straightway capable of rising to the still higher level of individuality in growth and in morality, nor to perceive and understand the unique nature which freedom chooses for herself in each individual. Most men rise but midway, expressing in fact only a raw elementary humanity, simply because they have not grasped the thought of their own higher being. As for me, it is this which has taken hold of me. The sense of freedom alone did not content me; it gave no meaning to my personality, nor to the peculiar unity of the transient stream of consciousness flowing within me, which urged me to seek something of higher ethical value of which it was the sign. I was not satisfied to view humanity in rough unshapen masses, inwardly altogether alike, and taking transient shape externally only by reason of mutual contact and friction.

Thus there dawned upon me what is now my highest intuition. I saw clearly that each man is meant to represent humanity in his own way, combining its elements uniquely, so that it may reveal itself in every mode, and all that can issue from its womb be made actual in the fullness of unending space and time. This thought alone has uplifted me, and set me apart from everything common and untransformed in my surroundings; it has made of me an elect creation of the godhead, rejoicing in a unique form and character. The act of freedom, which accompanied this inspiration has assembled and integrated the elements of human nature to make a unique existence. Had I from that time on surveyed the unique in my activity as constantly as I have always looked upon the universally human aspect of it, had I taken conscious possession of every action and limitation which were the consequence of that initial act of free determination, and had I given undisturbed attention to the further development of my unique nature and to each expression thereof, I could have no further doubt which province of humanity is mine, nor where to seek for the common principle which governs both the extension and the limitations of my growth. I should then have measured accurately the whole content of my being, ascertained my boundaries at every point, and should have known prophetically what I might yet be and might become. But tardily and only with great difficulty, does man reach the full knowledge of his individuality. He does not always dare to look toward it as his ideal, but prefers to turn his eyes upon the good which he possesses in common with humanity in general. Clinging to this common good with love and gratitude, he often doubts whether he should again separate his individual self from it. Confusing the sensuous with the spiritual, he fears lest he sink back into that culpably limited kind of external personality which preceded his new insight, and not until late does he learn to value and rightly use his highest privilege. Thus interrupted the consciousness of individuality must for a long time remain vacillating. The most characteristic efforts of one's nature often go unobserved, and when its limitations are most clearly apparent, the eye too readily skims over them, and fastens on something universal, where it might have found the unique by reason of its very limitations. However, I may be content with the way my will has conquered inertia, and practice trained my eye so that little now escapes it. Whenever I now act in keeping with my own spirit and disposition, my imagination gives me the clearest proof that I do so by free, individual choice, in suggesting to me a thousand other ways of acting in a different spirit, yet all also consistent with the universal laws of humanity. I project myself into a thousand different likenesses in order to behold my own more clearly.

But since the picture of my individuality does not yet present itself to me complete in all its features and is not yet certified by an unbroken continuity of clear self-consciousness, I am not yet able to maintain an attitude of unvarying, tranquil assurance in my self-contemplation. Often I must deliberately review all my efforts and actions, recall my history; nor must I disregard the opinions of my friends, whom I have gladly suffered to look into the depths of my inner life, if they differ from my own judgment. It is true that in my own eyes I still seem to be the same man I was when my higher life began, only more firm and more defined. And, indeed, how should a man, having once attained an independent and unique character, suddenly take on another nature in the very midst of his development and cultivation? How could he appropriate another side of human nature without having brought the first to its perfection? How could he wish to do it? And how could it occur without his knowing it? Either I have never understood myself, or I am still the person I believed myself to be, and every seeming contradiction, when solved by self-scrutiny, must reveal more clearly where and how the various strands of my own being are concealed and intertwined.

I am convinced that there is a two-fold vocation of men on earth, and it still seems to me to mark a great dichotomy in human nature. To develop one's inner humanity into distinctness, expressing it in manifold acts, is one thing, to project it into works of art which clearly convey to everyone who looks at them whatever their creator intended to show, is a totally different thing. He who is still on the lowest level, in the vestibule of uniqueness, fearing to limit himself by further decision, may seek to combine both courses with the result that he will not go far in either direction. Whosoever would really attain the one must let the other go. Not till the very end of life's development is there a bridge from one to the other, and it is open only to perfection such as man seldom reaches. How could I ever be in doubt as to my own choice? I have so emphatically eschewed everything that makes the artist; I have so eagerly made my own whatever serves the culture of the self, whatever hastens and confirms its development. The artist is on the alert for whatsoever may serve as sign and symbol of humanity; he ransacks the treasury of language and builds a world of music from a chaos of sound; he searches for a hidden meaning and a harmony in nature's lovely play of colors. In any work which he conceives he first investigates the effect of every part and searches out the law and structure of the whole, rejoicing more in the artistic vessel than in its costly content. Thereafter, ideas rise in his mind and shape themselves into new artistic creations; secretly he cherishes them in his soul; they grow in hidden silence. His productive energy knows no rest; he passes from project to execution and from execution to project; through constant practice his skill improves steadily; his riper judgment gives rein and check unto his fancy. This is the way that a creative nature advances toward the goal of perfection.

But all this I learned by observation, for it is alien to my thought. The humanity represented in a work of art stands out much more luminous and clear to me than the artist's artistry. The latter I get only with effort and later study, and then only enough to understand it a little. I like nature's free artistry just as it is; her lovely and meaningful signs awaken impressions and ideas in me without the impulse to force them into a more constricted form of my own creation. I do not insist upon a perfect treatment of the material in which my thought is expressed. And therefore I refrain from acquiring the utmost skill by practice, and when I have once put forth in action what is within me, I care not whether the act be often renewed in fairer and clearer fashion. Leisure is my dear divinity; by her favor man learns to understand and to determine himself. It is in leisure that ideas ripen unto power which easily governs all when the world calls for action. It follows also that I cannot work in isolation like the artist; in solitude the juices of my spirit are dried up, my thought stands still. I must go forth and enter into manifold association with others in order to behold what types of humanity there are, which of them are still alien to me, which I can assimilate, ever determining my own being more decidedly by mutual give and take. My unquenched thirst for ever continuing self-development does not permit me to give the expression of my inner life an external finish. I simply launch my word and deed upon the world, nothing mindful whether observers have the sense to penetrate a crude exterior and happily to find the inner meaning, the unique spirit even in its less perfect manifestations. I have neither time nor inclination for this; I must be up and doing, moving on beyond my last position, bringing my own being to its completion, if that be possible in this short life, through new activity and thought. I hate even to try the same thing twice, so little is there of the artist in me. Hence, everything I do, I like to do in the company of others; even while engaged in meditation, in contemplation, or in the assimilation of anything new, I need the presence of some loved one, so that the inner event may immediately be communicated, and I may forthwith make my account with the world through the sweet and easy mediation of friendship. So was it, so is it now, and I am still so distant from my goal that I should be mistaken in thinking it will ever be otherwise. Surely I am right, whatever friends may say, in excluding myself from the territory sacred to artists. Gladly do I renounce everything with which they have credited me, provided only that I find myself less imperfect than they imagine in the field where I have taken up my stand.

Reveal thyself to me once more, oh fair vision of that wide realm of humanity, where dwell all those who seek only to realize themselves, and to express themselves in manifold activities, without creating any permanent monument of their labor! Reveal thyself once more, and let me see whether a place of my own belongs to me in thy realm. Let me behold whether there is coherence within me, or whether some intrinsic contrarieties prevent the image of myself from closing into unity, so that my own being like some miscarried sketch instead of attaining its perfection dissolves into emptiness and unreality. O no, I need not fear, no sad presentiment of failure possesses my soul! I recognize that all within me articulates to form a genuine whole, no foreign element in my nature oppresses me, no organ is missing, nor any member eligible for my unique life. Whoever would make of himself a distinctive individual must be keen to perceive what he is not. For here, too, even in the realm of morality at its highest, that intimate connection between action and the perception of truth obtains. Only if man is conscious of his individuality in his present conduct can he be sure of not violating it in his next act, and only if he requires himself constantly to survey the whole of humanity, opposing his own expression of it to every other possible one, can he maintain the consciousness of his unique selfhood. For contrast is indispensable to set the individuality in relief. The highest condition of individual perfection in a limited field is a general sensitiveness. And how can this subsist apart from love? Without love, the very first attempt at self-formation would prove shattering because of the frightful disproportion between giving and receiving; the mind would be forced to some extreme one-sidedness, and he who made the attempt in this fashion would either be wholly broken or else sink to the vulgar level. Love, thou force of gravitation in the spiritual world, no individual life and no development is possible without thee! Without thee all things would flow together in a crude and homogeneous mass! Those who do not care to rise above this condition have little need of you; law and duty suffice for them, uniformity in conduct, and justice. For such as these the sacred sense of love would be a useless treasure, and this is why they let the little of it that they have grown wild, uncultivated. Not recognizing its sacredness, they cast it carelessly into the common pool of human goods, that should be governed according to a universal law. But for us, O love, thou art the alpha and omega. No development without love, and without individual development no perfection in love; each supplements the other, both increase indivisibly. I feel both of the highest conditions of morality united within me! I have made both sensitiveness and love my own, and both are ever waxing, a sure sign that my life is fresh and healthy, and that my individuality will develop more. Is there anything that lies beyond the range of my sensitiveness? Those who would have every one become a virtuoso and expert in some field of knowledge are wont to complain of me, that I will not suffer myself to be pinned down, that it is useless to hope I should ever seriously devote myself to some one thing. They say that when I have succeeded in gaining a certain view of things, my mind hastens on in its usual, restless, superficial fashion to other objects. Would that they leave me in peace, understanding that this is my destiny, that I must not devote myself to science, because I am set upon the development of myself! Would that they allowed me to keep my mind open toward all their busy endeavors, considering what I fashion within me as I contemplate their activities worth while their trouble! And yet their very complaints witness in my behalf. For there are others who are likewise dissatisfied with me, but for the opposite reason. These while unlike me in nature are nevertheless like me seeking to penetrate into the very center of humanity. They say my appreciation is fundamentally limited, that I can pass by indifferent to many sacred things, and spoil my deep innocent insight by vain contentiousness. Yes, I do still pass by much, but not with indifference. I dispute, but only to maintain my vision clear and open. Whenever I feel conscious of some expression of humanity that I have not mastered, my first concern is to dispute, not indeed whether it exists, but whether it is of such a nature, and only such, as is shown me by him in whom I first encounter it. My late awakened spirit, remembering how long it bore an alien yoke, fears ever lest it be subjected again to the domination of some alien opinion, and whenever a strange object discloses a new aspect of life, my first step is to rise in arms against it, in order to fight for freedom and not to fall back at every new experience into the slavery in which my education began. As soon, however, as I have won my distinctive point of view, the time for strife is over, and I gladly suffer each other view to take its place beside my own; my mind in peace completes the work of penetrating and interpreting each other standpoint.

Thus it is, that what may often seem a limitation of my sensitiveness is really but the first stir of appreciation within me. To be sure, I have very often had to assert myself positively, during this beautiful time of my life, when I came into contact with so much that was new to me, when so much became broad daylight to me which I had but darkly sensed before, and for which I had no preparation! Often I was obliged to appear antagonistic to those who were a source of new insight for me. Unperturbed I have suffered their misapprehension, trusting that they would understand, as soon as they had entered more deeply into my nature. Even my friends have frequently misunderstood me in this way, especially when I passed by unsympathetically, though not with enmity, things which ardently appealed to them and excited their zeal. The mind cannot apprehend all things at once: it is useless for it to try to finish its task by a single effort; its process must be continuous in two directions, and each man has his own way of combining both in order to make up the whole. For me it is impossible, when anything new presents itself, to penetrate at once into its core with burning intensity and get to know it perfectly. Such an attempt would ill beseem that equanimity which is the keynote of my being's harmony. To seize upon some such particular would upset the balance of my life, and while I became absorbed in that one thing I should lose contact with the rest, without even making the first truly my own. I must first store up every new acquisition in my mind, and then let the usual forces of my life play upon it and about it, so that the new shall be mingled with the old, and come into touch with everything that I already harbor within me. Only by such activity as this do I succeed in preparing the way for a deeper and more intimate perception; contemplation and practice must often alternate before I am satisfied that I have fathomed anything. Thus and thus alone can I go about my business, if I am not to violate my inner being, for in me self-development and activity turned beyond the self must balance at every moment. Therefore my progress is slow, and I shall have to live long before I have embraced all things equally, but whatever I do embrace will bear my impress. Whatever part of humanity's infinite realm I have apprehended will be in equal measure uniquely transformed and taken up into my being.

Oh how much richer my life has become! What sweet awareness of inner worth; what enhanced assurance of individuality rewards me when I survey the profit of so many happy and prosperous days! My silent effort, though it appear like mere idleness from without, was not in vain; it has well served my inward task of self-development. Mistaken outward activity ill-suited to my nature would not have carried this so far, and restricting the range of my appreciation would have impeded it still more. Alas that a man's inner character should be so misjudged, even by those who might understand and who deserve to recognize it everywhere! Alas that so many, even of these, confuse outward behavior and inner activity, deeming it possible to construe the latter like the former from fragmentary appearances, and suspecting contradiction where everything fits to perfection! Is then my real character so hard to recognize? Am I ever to forego my heart's dearest desire to show myself as I am to all my worthy fellow men? For even now, as I look deeply into my nature, I am confirmed anew in the conviction that this is the strongest motive in my being. This is the truth, no matter how often I am told that I am shut up in myself, and that I often coldly repel the hallowed advances of love and friendship. To be sure, I never deem it necessary to talk of what I have done or what has happened to me. In my view, the worldly part of me is too insignificant that I should weary by dwelling on it, those whom I would gladly wish to have know me inwardly. Nor do I care to speak of that which is still dark and unformed within me lacking that clarity which makes it mine. How should I offer to my friend what does not yet belong to me? Why thereby hide from him what I already am? How could I hope to communicate, without raising up misunderstanding, that which I do not yet understand myself? Such an attitude on my part does not argue reticence and lack of love. Rather is it the evidence of a holy reverence without which there is no real love; it is the instinct of delicacy that would not profane the highest, nor needlessly obscure it. As soon as I have genuinely appropriated anything new in respect to culture and individuality, from whatever source, do I not run to my friend in word and deed to let him know of it, that he may share my joy, and himself profit as he perceives understandingly my inner growth? My friend I cherish as my own self; whatever I come to recognize as my own, I place straightway at his disposal. It is true I sometimes take less interest than do those who call themselves his friends in what he does and in that which happens to him. His outward behavior neither affects nor concerns me, if I already understand the inner being whence it flows, and know that it must of necessity be thus, because my friend is such as he is. This outward side of him neither feeds nor excites my love for him, has no relation to it. It belongs to the world and with all its consequences must conform to the laws of necessity. But whatever the consequences, whatever happens to my friend, he will surely know how to act with a freedom worthy of himself. And nothing else concerns me. I contemplate his fate with calmness even as I do my own. Who will regard this as cold indifference? A clear appreciation of the contrast between world and man is the ground on which all self-respect and sense of freedom rest. Should I grant this less unto my friend than unto myself?

This is the very thing of which I chiefly boast, that my love and friendship always have so high a source, that they have never been blended with any vulgar sentiment, have never been the offspring of habit or tender feeling, but ever an act of purest freedom, orientated towards the individuality of other human beings. I have ever kept the more common sentiment at a distance from myself. A benefit has never bribed me into friendship, nor has beauty stolen my love. Pity has never so enmeshed my judgment that it ascribed a merit to misfortune and represented suffering human beings as otherwise and better than they are. And so a place was cleared in my soul for genuine love and friendship, and my longing to fill this space with ever larger and more manifold content never abates. Wherever I notice an aptitude for individuality, inasmuch as love and sensitiveness, its highest guarantees, are present, there I also find an object for my love. I would have my love embrace every unique self, from the unsophisticated youth, in whom freedom is but beginning to germinate, to the ripest and most finished type of man. Whenever I see such a one, I give him the salutation of the love within me, even if our brief meeting and parting permit no more than this gesture of spiritual greeting. Neither do I measure my friendship for anyone by any worldly standard of external appearances. My vision soars beyond the worldly and temporal, seeking inner greatness. Whether he to whom I would be a friend is already sensitive to much or little, whether he is or is not far advanced in his development, whether he has many achievements to his credit or not, all these things may not determine my attitude toward him, and whatever is missing in this respect I can easily dispense with. His unique being and its relation to humanity is the object of my quest. I love him in the measure that I find and understand this individuality, but I can give him proof thereof only in proportion to his understanding of my own true self. Alas, often did this love of mine return to me uncomprehended, the language of the heart was not heard, as if I had remained dumb, and those to whom I would have shown my love actually believed I had.

Men often travel in neighboring ways, and yet are not near each other. The one divines a friendly presence and is inclined toward friendly greeting. He calls but calls in vain; the other does not hear him. Frequently opposites approach each other, and henceforth there is to be no more separation. But their encounter is for a moment only, and movements in opposite directions sweep them from each other's ken, neither knowing whither the other has disappeared. This has often befallen me in my longing for love. Would it not be shameful, if I had not at last been disciplined, if my all too easy optimism had not fled, and experienced wisdom taken its place? "Here is one who will understand you in part, there another who will understand a different side of you; a certain kind of love is possible toward the one, but beware how you offer it to the other." Thus am I often vainly warned to be discreet. For the urge of my heart leaves little room for prudence; much less can I presume to assign limits to other men, and to say how far they should respond to me and to my love. I always take too much for granted, I always try again, and am forthwith punished for my avarice by losing what I had already gained. But no other fortune is possible for one who is engaged in forming himself, and that I suffer thus is the surest proof that I am so engaged. A person so occupied, uniquely combines in himself various elements of humanity. He belongs to more than one world. How could he move in an orbit exactly parallel to that of another, who is also a distinctive individual, how continue in his neighborhood? Like a comet the cultured individual traverses many systems and encircles many a sun. Now he passes a certain star which sees him gladly, and seeks to know him; he on his part bends his course with friendly intent in that star's direction. Then lo! he has moved away into far-off spaces, his very shape seems changed; there is a doubt whether he is still the same. But anon he returns in swift revolution and there takes place anew a passing interchange of love and friendship. But where find the fair ideal of complete and permanent union, of friendship perfect on both sides? Only where on both sides love and sensitiveness have increased in equal measure as it were beyond all measure. But then, in such a perfect love the individuals themselves are also made perfect. The hour is at hand—ah! for all of us it strikes much sooner—to yield up finite existence, and to return out of the world to the bosom of the infinite.

The World

DREAR OLD AGE, THEY say, has the right to complain about the world; it may be pardoned for preferring to look back on better days when life was at the full. Joyous youth should smile upon life, ignoring defects, making the most of what is there, and trusting readily to the sweet deceits of hope. But the truth, a correct estimate of the world, is credited to him alone, who secure in the contentment of middle age, neither vainly grieves nor falsely hopes. Such contentment, however, is but folly's passage from hope in life to contempt for it; such wisdom but the hollow echo of footsteps reluctantly moving on from youth to age; such satisfaction is a stupid turn of make-believe courtesy on the part of one who would escape outright impeachment of a world, in which his stay is bound to be soon cut short, and who would no less avoid impeaching his own judgment; such praise of middle-life is vanity ashamed of its mistakes, it is a forgetting of recent desires, it is the complacency which contents itself with poverty rather than submit to toil. I did not flatter myself when I was young, and therefore, I do not flatter the world now, nor at any time. It cannot disappoint one who expects nothing, nor will he offend it in revenge. I have done little to make things what they are, and so I need not expect to find them better. Nothing disgusts me more than the vile praise, which is lavished on the world from all sides, by those who wish to shine in the reflected light of their own handiwork. This perverse generation loves to talk of how it has improved the world, in order to plume itself and to be considered superior to its ancestors. Were perfected human nature already in blossom and diffusing its first sweet fragrance, were the seeds of self-culture for ever so many individuals already assured of their growth on the soil of a common civilization, if the breath of every life were already free and sacred, and if a pervasive love drew all humanity into miraculous relationships ever productive of new and marvelous fruit, even then this generation could not outdo its glittering praise of mankind's present estate. To hear them discourse on the world of today, one would imagine the thundering voice of their mighty reason had burst the chains of ignorance, that they had at last succeeded in setting up a perfect portrait of human nature, which formerly had been painted obscurely in colors of darkness so as to be scarcely recognizable, but which now was marvelously illumined by light from above, so that no sane vision could longer mistake the general outlines or even the individual traits; they speak as if the music of their wisdom had transformed raw, predatory self-seeking into the tamest house-pet and taught it the arts. Every least moment is supposed to have been full of progress. O how deeply I despise this generation, which plumes itself more shamelessly than any previous one ever did, which can scarcely endure the belief in a still better future and reviles everyone who dedicates himself thereto, simply because the true goal of mankind, toward which the age has risked scarcely a single step, lies unknown to it in the dim distance!

Of course, if one is content to have man control the material world alone, tapping all its powers for his own service, and conquering space so that it no longer cripples the strength of his spirit, the mere nod of his will instantly and everywhere producing the action it intends, with all things under the dominion of ideas and the spirit's presence everywhere revealed; whoever is content to see crude matter vitalized and to have mankind find the joy of living in the consciousness of mastering its body,—let him, for whom this is the ultimate aim, join in the noisy praise of our times. For now as never before may man justly boast such mastery. However much remains undone, enough has been accomplished to make him feel lord of the earth, believing that nothing may be left unattempted in this, his own particular domain, and that the concept of impossibility, ever narrowing, must finally vanish altogether. In respect to this purpose I feel that communion with mankind augments my own powers in every moment of my life. Each of us plies his own particular trade, completing the work of someone whom he never knew, or preparing the way for another who in turn will scarcely recognize how much he owes to him. Thus the work of humanity is promoted throughout the world; everyone feels the influence of others as part of his own life; by the ingenious mechanism of this community the slightest movement of each individual is conducted like an electric spark, through a long chain of a thousand living links, greatly amplifying its final effect; all are, as it were, members of a great organism, and whatever they may have done severally, is instantaneously consummated as its work. Probably this sense of life's enhancement by common effort is more vividly and more satisfyingly present in me than in those who are so loud in its praise. For I am not disturbed and disappointed by their gloomy supposition that the gains, which all helped to produce and to maintain are enjoyed so unequally. Lazy thinking and emptiness of mind can be but a loss to anyone, habit. levies it, tax on us all, and whenever I compare a person's restrictions with his powers, I arrive at the same ratio, expressing in different ways an equal measure of life for all. But even so I regard this whole sense of a common material progress to be of little value; it is not further gain in this direction that I desire for the world; it causes me mortal agony that this, an unholy waste of its holy powers, should be regarded as mankind's entire task. My demands are not so modest as to be content with the improvement of man's relation to external nature, even though this relation were already brought to the highest point of perfection! Is man then merely a creature of the senses, for whom a heightened feeling of vitality, of health and strength can be the highest good? Is the spirit satisfied to inhabit the body, extending and augmenting its powers in conscious mastery thereof? For this is the multitude's whole ambition, and upon such achievements they base their unmeasured pride. From caring for their own physical existence and well-being they have come to care for the similar well-being of all, but that is as far as they have risen in their consciousness of humanity. That is what virtue, justice, and love mean to them; that is the essence of their noisy triumph over base self-seeking; that is the end of all their wisdom, and such are the only links they are able to break in the chain of ignorance; everybody is to cooperate and every association is to be formed for an aim no higher than this. O what a perversion to think a man should devote his spiritual powers to secure for others what he himself spurns as inferior! How disfigured the mind which deems it a virtue to sacrifice the highest in such low idolatry!

Accept thy harsh lot, O my soul, to have seen the light only in such dark and wretched days. You can hope for naught from such a world to further your aspirations, it offers nothing for your inner development! You will necessarily find association with it a limitation, rather than an enhancement of your powers. All who know the higher ambitions experience this. Many a human heart thirsts for love; many a man is haunted by the image of an ideal companion with whom close interchange of thought and feeling would prove mutually profitable and elevating, but unless perchance he discovers such a friend within his own narrow circle, both he and that other consume their brief lives in a mutual longing! The earth's resources and their location are described by thousands; I can learn in a moment where any material thing I need is to be found, and in the next I can possess it. But no means exists for discovering such a personality, as is indispensable to the nurture of my inner life. Society is not organized for such a purpose; to bring together those who need each other is no one's business. And even if he, whose heart seeks love everywhere in vain, should learn where dwelt his friend and his beloved, yet would he be restricted by his station in life, by the rank which he holds in that meagre thing we call society. Man clings to these restricting ties more tenaciously than stone or plant to mother earth. The piteous fate of the negro, torn from his loved ones and his native land, for base servitude in a strange and distant country, is daily meted out in the routine of the world to better men also, who, prevented from reaching the distant homeland where dwell their unfound friends, must waste away their inner lives ineffectually in surroundings that ever remain alien and barren to them. Many a man has sufficient penetration to apprehend the inner meaning of human nature, he is prepared to discriminate its various forms and to find what is common to them, but it chances that he lives in a barren wilderness or amid unfruitful luxuriance, where the everlasting monotony gives no nourishment to his spirit's needs. Thus driven inward upon itself his imagination sickens, his spirit is forced to consume itself in dreamy fictions, for the world offers him no sustenance. It is no one's business to supply him with the sustenance he needs, or to take an interest in placing him in a more favorable atmosphere. Again, many a man has a genuine impulse to create works of art, but opportunity to sift his materials, to discard carefully and successfully all that is out of keeping is denied him. Or, if his project does achieve unity and fair proportions, he may lack opportunity to give its details the last touch of perfection. Does anyone furnish what he lacks, or freely offer him counsel, or take active part in perfecting his unfinished work? On the contrary, each man must stand alone and attempt the impossible! Neither in art nor in the realization of human perfection is there community of talent, such as was instituted long ago for the service of man's external needs! The artist becomes aware of other men's existence only when pained by criticisms irrelevant to his genius, or when their deficient understanding thwarts the effect of his own esthetic intent. Thus in his highest concerns man seeks help in vain from association with his fellow-beings, and even to expect such aid is exasperating and foolish in the estimations of the elect of our age. To presage a higher, more intimate, spiritual community, to wish to promote it despite limited outlooks and petty prejudices seems to them vain romanticism. If one feels oppressed by life's limitations, they attribute it to misplaced idealism and not to life's poverty; culpable inertia, they claim, and not a lack of social encouragement is what makes a man dissatisfied with the world and disposes him to let his empty wishes roam over vast tracts of the impossible. Impossible! yes, for him whose vision is on the low plane of the present with its small horizon. What grievous doubts would assail me of man's ability to draw nearer his goal, if by weakness of imagination I were riveted to the actual and its immediate consequences.

All who belong to a better world must for the present pine in dismal servitude! Whatever spiritual association now exists is debased in service of the earthly; aimed at some utility it confines the spirit and does violence to the inner life. When friends extend to each other the hand of fellowship, the bond should issue in something greater than each could achieve independently; each ought to grant the other full play to follow the promptings of his spirit, offering assistance only where the other feels a lack, and not insinuating his own ideas in place of his friend's. In this wise each would find life and strength in the other, and the potentialities within him would be fully realized. But what, on the other hand, comes to pass in the world? There is always some one ready to perform material service for another, even ready to sacrifice his own wellbeing, while to exchange knowledge, to show sympathy, to mitigate sufferings, is what ranks as the highest. But there is ever an element of antipathy to the inner nature of man in ordinary friendships; people would like to have certain faults cancelled out of a friend's character, and what would be a fault in themselves they regard as such in him, too. Thus each makes sacrifice of his individuality to suit the other, until they become alike, but neither like his own true self, unless one of them has will enough to check this ruination, or unless, after long suspense between strife and concord, the friendship weakens and dissolves. Woe to the man of yielding disposition, if a friend becomes attached to him! He, poor fellow, dreams of a new and stronger life, he rejoices in the happy hours which pass sweetly in this comradeship and little does he see how his spirit becomes involved in this false felicity, and dissipates itself until at last his inner life, injured and crushed at every point, is obliterated. Many of the better sort have come to this pass, the fundamental traits of their own natures are scarcely recognizable any longer, mutilated as they are at the hand of friends and plastered all over with unnatural affectations. Man and wife are united in tender affection, and go to build themselves a home. Even as new individuals issue from the lap of their love, so too a new and common will should develop from the harmony of their natures. Their peaceful home with its occupations, its arrangements and private joys, should reveal this will in action. Alas! that this finest of human relationships should be so universally desecrated! Its true significance remains a closed secret to those that enter into it; each keeps and cultivates his own will after marriage as before, they take turns in governing, and in silent disappointment each reckons up whether the gain really outweighs what he has sacrificed in sheer freedom. At last each becomes the other's fate, and confronting cold necessity, the ardor of their love dies out. In the last analysis, when measured by the same standard, all men's accounts come equally to nought. Every home should be the beautiful embodiment, the fine creation of a unique soul; it should have its own stamp and unique characteristics, but with a dumb monotony they are all a desolate grave of freedom and true life. Does she make him happy? Does she live for him alone? Does he make her happy? Is he all complaisance? Do both count mutual sacrifice their highest joy? O torture me not, image of misery which I see deep hid behind their bliss, a sign of nearby death, the wonted deceiver who paints before them this last counterfeit of life!—What has become of the fables of ancient sages about the state? Where is the power with which this highest level of existence should endow mankind, where the consciousness each should have of partaking in the state's reason, its imagination, and its strength? Where is devotion to this new existence that man has conceived, a will to sacrifice the old individual soul rather than lose the state, a readiness to set one's life at stake rather than see the fatherland perish? Where is foresight keeping close watch lest the country be seduced and its spirit corrupted? Where find the individual character each state should have, and the acts that reveal it? The present generation is so far from even suspecting what this side of humanity signifies, that it dreams of reorganizing the state as it does of human ideals in general; each, whether he lives in one of the old or new states, would pour all into his own mold, like some sage who lays down a model for the future in his works, and hopes that one day all mankind will venerate it as the symbol of its salvation. They all believe that the best of states is one that gives least evidence of its existence, and that permits the need for which it exists to be least in evidence also. Whoever thus regards the greatest achievement of human art, by which man should be raised to the highest level of which he is capable, as nothing but a necessary evil, as an indispensable mechanism for covering up crime and mitigating its effects, must inevitably sense nothing but a limitation in that which is designed to enhance his life in the highest degree.

O what is the vile source of these great evils but the fact that man has no sense for anything but visible, external association, and that he wants to mold and measure everything in terms of this? In so far as association is external, it must always involve limitation. The man who would amass material possessions must grant others opportunity for doing likewise; the sphere occupied by each sets a limit to the rest, and they respect it only because they are not able to possess the world individually, but can make use of each other's persons and goods. All else is concentrated upon this one end: increase in outward possessions or in knowledge, aid and protection against fate or misfortune, stronger alliances to keep rivals in check. This is all that men nowadays seek and find in friendship, marriage, and fatherland; they do not seek what they need to supplement their own efforts toward self-development, nor enrichment of the inner life. In respect to such ends every association that one enters into, from the very earliest educational ties onward, is a hindrance; at the very outset the youthful spirit, instead of enjoying free play and opportunity to see world and man as a whole, is restricted by alien ideas and early accustomed to a life of prolonged spiritual slavery. In the midst of wealth what lamentable poverty! How unavailing is the struggle of a superior mind, seeking moral cultivation and development, with this world that recognizes only legality, that offers dead formulas in place of life, custom and routine in place of free activity, a world that boasts of great wisdom when, happily, some outworn form is discarded and gives place to something new that seems vital at the moment, but which will all too soon become a mere formula and lifeless convention in its turn. How should I find salvation in such a world were it not for you, divine imagination! Did not you give me the certain premonition of better times to come!

Yes, culture will develop out of barbarism, and life will spring even from the sleep of death! The elements of a better life are already present. Their superior potency will not remain forever in dormant hiding; sooner or later the spirit dwelling in man will arouse them into activity. As the cultivation of the earth for man's benefit is now far superior to that crude dominion over nature, wherein men fled timidly before every manifestation of her powers, so the blessed time when a true and spiritual society shall arise cannot be remote from this present childhood of humanity. The rude slave of nature would have believed nothing of a future dominion over her, nor would he have understood what had inspired the soul of one who prophesied thereof, for he lacked even the conception of this condition for which he felt no desire. Just so the man of today, if anyone holds up to him unfamiliar ideals or speaks of a different society and different relationships, cannot conceive of anything better or higher for which one could wish, nor is he at all fearful of anything ever coming to pass that would deeply put to shame his pride and indolent complacency. Yet if our present, much vaunted enlightenment developed out of a wretched barbarism, in which the germs of progress are scarcely discernible even now to a vision trained by the subsequent course of events, why should not our chaotic philistinism, amid which the eye already discerns through sinking mists the rudiments of a better world, give place at last to the sublime rule of moral and spiritual cultivation. It is coming! Why should I with faint heart count the hours which must still transpire or the generations that must pass away ere then? Wyly let the time of its coming trouble me, since time does not comprehend my inner life?

A man belongs to the world he helped to create; his will and his thought are all absorbed in it, and it is outside its bounds that he is a stranger. Whoever lives at peace with the present and desires nothing further is a contemporary of those semi-barbarous people who laid the foundations of our world; his life is a sequel to theirs, he is satisfied to enjoy the fulfillment of their wishes, and a better condition which they could not conceive, he does not conceive either. I, for my part, am a stranger to the life and thought of this present generation, I am a prophet-citizen of a later world, drawn thither by a vital imagination and strong faith; to it belong my every word and deed. What the present world is doing and undergoing leaves me unmoved; far below me it appears insignificant, and I can at a glance survey the confused course of its great revolutions. Through every revolution whether in the field of science or of action it returns ever to the same point, and presenting ever the same features clearly reveals its limitations and the narrow scope of its endeavors. Its own works are impotent to advance it; they but keep it going in the same old cycle, and hence I can take no delight in them; I am not deceived into placing false hope in everything that appears to contain some promise. But wherever I do see a spark of the hidden fire that must sooner or later consume the outworn and recreate the world, I am drawn toward it with love and true hope as to a welcome sign of my distant home. And close at hand the sacred flame has appeared shedding its unearthly light, a sign, to the knowing, that the spirit is there. All who like myself belong to the future are drawing toward each other in love and hope, and each in his every word and act cements and extends a spiritual bonus by which we are pledged to better times.

But this too the world makes as difficult as possible; it prevents kindred minds from recognizing each other, and contrives thus to destroy the seed of future improvement. An act, born of the most immaculate conception, is nevertheless subject to a thousand misinterpretations; it is inevitable that what has been done in the purest moral spirit should often be associated with worldly motives. Too many mask themselves in false appearances to allow of confidence in everyone who shows signs of superior spirit. It is right to be skeptical of first appearances when looking for brothers in spirit; yet because the world and the times make ready confidence impossible, it often happens that two congenial spirits pass each other by unrecognized. Knowing this, take courage and have hope! You are not the only one whose roots strike into that deeper soil which at some distant time will be the surface; the seed of the future is germinating everywhere! Continue to look for it wherever possible. You will still find many a friend and will learn to recognize as such many whom you have long misjudged. And you yourself will be recognized by many; despite the world, mistrust and suspicion will at last disappear, if by the constancy of your action you give a steady token to the pure in heart. You need but impress the spirit's stamp incisively upon every action, that those who are near may discover you. Only pronounce clearly the sentiment of your heart, that those who are distant may hear!

To be sure, the world, again, has the magic of language at its command, and we have not. Language has exact symbols in fine abundance for everything thought and felt in the world's sense; it is the clearest mirror of the times, a work of art revealing the current spirit. But for our purposes language is still crude and undeveloped, a poor instrument of communion. O how long at the outset it hinders the spirit from arriving at an immediate vision of itself! Before it has yet found itself the spirit is enmeshed in the world through language, and its first difficulty is to gradually extricate itself from this entanglement. And if in spite of all the errors and corruptions introduced by words, the spirit has at last penetrated through to truth, how treacherously language then changes her tactics, now isolating and imprisoning its victim, so that he cannot communicate his discovery, nor receive further sustenance from the outside. Long must he search amid the profusion of language before a term can be found, above all suspicion, to which his inmost thought can be entrusted; once found the unspiritual immediately catch up the phrase, give it some strange twist, so that a person hearing it thereafter must needs doubt as to its original connections. Many a word comes in answer from a distance to such an isolated soul, but he must question whether it really means what it means to him, whether it was sent by friend or foe. Is then language indeed the common possession of the children of the spirit and the children of the world! How absurd that the latter should pretend to an interest in true wisdom! No, they shall not succeed either in confusing or intimidating us! We are here waging a great battle around the sacred standard of humanity, which we, men of the future, must maintain for the coming generations. It is a decisive battle, but also a certain victory, to be won, independent of chance or fortune, by spiritual strength and genuine art.

Manners should be the outer garment worn by inner individuality, delicately and significantly adapted to its form, revealing its fine proportions and gracefully following its movement. Always treat this consummate investiture with piety, giving it ever a lighter and finer texture, drawing it ever more closely about the self. Then must hypocrisy at length come to end, for a profane and vulgar nature appearing in the guise of nobility will soon be exposed. The informed observer will at every movement detect concealed defects, the magic raiment will fall loosely where there is emptiness, and betray inward unshapeliness by its flutter at every rapid step. Thus the constancy and evenness of one's bearing ought to become and will become an infallible criterion of the spiritual nature within, and a token by which superior minds privately recognize each other. Language too should objectify the most interior thoughts, the highest intuitions, the most hidden observations of the spirit upon its own conduct, and the marvelous music of words should indicate the value, the degree of love, attached to each object. For though others can abuse the symbols which we consecrate to the highest, and can insinuate their petty and limited meanings where the reference is to the holy, yet is the tone of the worldling different from that of the consecrated. The same intellectual symbols dispose themselves differently and suggest a different melody to the wise than to the slaves of the age; the latter elevate something else to a first principle, and arrive at consequences that to the former are remote and strange. Each of us need only make his language thoroughly his own and artistically all of a piece, so that its derivation and modulation, its logic and its sequences, exactly represent the structure of his spirit, and the music of his speech has the accent of his heart and the keynote of his thought. If we do this, there will appear within the vulgar tongue another language, secret and holy, which the unconsecrated can neither interpret nor imitate, because the key to its characters lies in its spiritual meaning; a few phrases of his thought, a few notes of his discourse will betray the outsider.

O if only the wise and the good might thus recognize each other by their manner and their language, if the present confusion were only dissolved and the issue clearly drawn, if the inner feud would only come to an open breach! Then victory too would draw nigh, a fairer sun would rise, for the younger generation with its open mind and unprejudiced spirit would surely incline to the better side. Significant actions can but announce the spirit's presence, and miracles must bear witness to an imprint of divine origin. It would then be evident that the absence of beauty and unity in one's bearing, or the assuming of manners as a frigid semblance to disguise deformity, betokens deficient awareness of inner reality. It would be evident that he knows nothing about self-cultivation and has never beheld in himself the essential man, for whom the foundation-stones of language, quarried out of the inner life, have weathered and broken into small fragments; whose eloquence, designed to touch the depths, evaporates into meaningless phrases and superficial polish, while its lofty music degenerates into idle tonal artifices that are impotent to represent the real character of the spirit. No one can live simply and in the way of beauty save he who hates lifeless formulas, seeks after genuine self-cultivation, and so belongs to a world that is yet to be. No one can become a true artist in the use of language save he who sees himself with unclouded insight and has made the inner nature of man his own.

It is the quiet omnipotence of these sentiments, and not the criminal violence of vain experimentation, that must at last produce reverence for the highest and the dawn of a better age. May it be the aim of my life to promote such reverence, and may I thereby discharge my obligations to the world and fulfill my calling. Thus will the power I exercise combine with the efforts of all the elect, and what issues from my nature as a free activity will help mankind on the way to its true goal.

Prospect

IT IS TRUE THAT we all walk the earth under the dispensation of powers not our own, and live uncertain of the future? Is it true that a heavy veil conceals every man's destiny, and that fate as a blind force, or even as the alien, arbitrary will of a higher Providence—for my purpose I see no distinction—plays with our decisions as with our desires? Certainly, if our decisions are no more than wishes, then man is the toy of chance! If he has learned to find himself nowhere but in the flux of those transient impressions and particular ideas that happen to be the realities of his life; if his whole life is preoccupied with the insecure possession of external things, and he never penetrates more deeply into his own being, because he is absorbed in dizzy contemplation of the everlasting swirl in which both he and his possessions are carried round; if under the influence of one random emotion or another his attention is always directed upon some particular external thing, which he wants to pursue or possess according to the impulse of the moment; then to be sure fate may prove hostile, robbing him of what he desires and playing with his resolutions, which deserve to be regarded as toys; then let him complain of uncertainty, since from his point of view nothing is certain; then indeed his own blindness must seem like a heavy veil, and it must surely be dark where the light of freedom does not shine; then, of course, he must want to know above all whether the changes that govern him are dependent on a supreme will above all wills, or whether they are a mechanical result of the combination of many forces. For this latter possibility must terrify one who has never laid hold of his true self. If every ray of light upon the infinite chaos of things shows man more clearly that he is not a free being, but only a cog in the great wheel which moves both him and all else in its eternal revolution, then hope, renewed again and again in defiance of all experience and all knowledge, hope in a sublime mercy must be his only support.

Welcome art thou, oh cherished assurance of freedom! Every time I see the slaves of necessity trembling I welcome thee anew! Oh the beauty and peace of that clear understanding with which I confidently greet the future, knowing what it is and what it has in store; I am its master, it is not mine. It hides nothing from me; it approaches without any pretense of power over me. Only the gods, who have no further scope for self-improvement, are ruled by fate, and the worst of mortals, who have no desire to perfect themselves, but not the man who is occupied, as he should be, in developing himself. Where find the limit set to my power? At what point does the dread realm of alien necessity begin? The only impossibility of which I am aware is to transcend the limits which I freely placed upon my nature from the beginning; the only things I cannot do are those which I surrendered in deciding what I wanted to become; naught else is impossible for me save to reverse that original decision as once taken. Whoever regards such limitation which is the essential condition of his very existence, of his freedom, of his having a will at all, as an alien coercion seems to me strangely confused. But do I sense any further restrictions upon me within the limits of my chosen sphere? Without doubt this would be the case, if even in matters of morality and self-culture I harbored the desire for some specific result at each moment; if the performance of some particular action should at any time become in itself the object of my will, then, to be sure, this object might escape me just when I wanted it. In such a case I should indeed find myself under alien control, but were I to blame fate, I should only be mistaking the real thing at fault, namely myself. But such a fate can never befall me! For I live always in the light of my entire being. My only purpose is ever to become more fully what I am; each of my acts is but a special phase in the unfolding of this single will; and no less certain than my power to act at all is my ability to act always in this spirit; in the sequence of my actions there will be nothing unconformable to this principle. Come then what may! My will rules fate, as long as I relate everything to this comprehensive purpose, and remain indifferent to external conditions and forms of life, considering them all as of equal value to me provided only that they express the nature of my being and afford new material for its inner cultivation and growth. As long as my spirit's eye keeps in view this object in its entirety, seeing each particular purpose only as contained in this whole, yet truly seeing in this whole all particular aims, as long as I never drop out of mind the pursuit that I happen to interrupt, keeping my will fixed upon more than I do, relating whatever I do to all that I will, just so long does my will rule fate, and freely turn to its purposes whatever fate may bring. Such a will can never be cheated of its object, and in its very conception the idea of fate vanishes. Whence then do those changes of human fortune, which men feel to be so tyrannous, take their rise but in the fact that freedom limits freedom in a community of such wills? Thus these changes are also an effect of freedom, and of my own freedom to boot. How could I suffer my actions to help form the vicissitudes of other men, if I did not demand that those of others should do the same for me? Yes, I do demand it most emphatically! Let time move on, and bring me what manifold materials it may for my activity, my self-development, and for the outward expression of my nature. I flinch at nothing, the order in which it comes is immaterial to me, and so are all the external conditions. Whatever the active community of mankind can produce shall pass before me, shall stir and affect me in order to be affected by me in turn, and in the manner I receive and treat it, I intend always to find my freedom and to develop my individuality through its outward expression.

Is this but a vain delusion? Does impotence hide behind this sense of freedom? Such is the interpretation which vulgar natures put upon a thing they do not understand! But this empty talk of men who debase themselves has long ago ceased to echo in my ears; between their point of view and mine the living fact renders judgment at every moment. When they see time passing, they always complain, and they tremble at an hour's approach! Through every change they pass unimproved, ever remaining the same vulgar natures that they are. But can they cite a single instance in which they might not have met the circumstances which confronted them differently? It would be easy for me to crush them still more in the midst of their troubles, forcing from them the contrite confession that the alien tyranny of which they complain is nothing but their own inertia, that they did not really want what they seemed to want, but only wished to appear desirous of it. Thus showing them the base limitations of their own consciousness and will, I might teach them to believe in a true will and true consciousness.

But whether they learn the truth or no, my own belief that I shall meet with nothing that can hinder the progress of my self-development or drive me from the goal of my endeavors, lives in me because of past acts. Ever since reason obtained the mastery of my being, and freedom and self-knowledge took up their abode in me, I have walked through diverse courses of life with this clear confidence. While enjoying the beautiful freedom of youth I succeeded in the crucial act of casting off the mummery in which long and tedious hours of educational sacrilege had clothed me; I learned to deplore the brief independence enjoyed by the majority of men who allow themselves to be bound by new chains; I learned to despise the contemptible efforts of the lifeless, who have forgotten even the last trace of the brief dream of freedom, who mistake what transpires in youth when freedom is just awakening and wish to keep the young faithful to old ways. In a stranger's home my sense for the beauty of human fellowship was first awakened; I saw that it requires freedom to ennoble and give right expression to the delicate intimacies of human nature, which remain forever obscure to the uninitiated who respect them only as natural bans. Amid all the diversities of this world's motley spectacle I learned to discount appearances and to recognize the same reality whatever its garb, and I also learned to translate the many tongues that it acquires in various circles. Watching the great ferments of life, both the turbulent and the quiet ones, I learned to understand the mentality of mankind, and how it cleaves ever to superficialities. In the quiet solitude that was my lot I looked to the inner nature of things, I took note of all purposes to which humanity is committed by its essence, and observed all dispositions of the spirit in their everlasting unity; through living contemplation I learned to assess at the right value the dead language of the schools. I have felt joy and pain, I know each sorrow and each smile, and in all that has happened to me since my real life began, is there anything from which my being did not gain strength or acquire something new, wherewith to nourish my inner life?

Let the past, therefore, be my security for the future. How can the future, being like the past, affect me differently if I remain constant to myself? I see the content of my life before me clear and fixed. I know in what respects my being has already achieved its individual form and definition, and by acting with thorough consistency on every hand, with full and undivided strength, I shall preserve what has thus been achieved. How can I help but rejoice in novelty and in variety, which but confirms in new and ever different ways the truth whereof I am possessed. Am I so certain of myself that I do not require such further confirmations? Am I so complete as not to welcome joy and sorrow alike, indeed whatever the world calls weal or woe, seeing that everything in its own way serves the purpose of further revealing my being's relationships? If but this be accomplished, of what importance is it that I be happy! Moreover, I also know what I have not yet made my own, I know where I am. still adrift amid vague generalities and for a long time have painfully felt the lack of an individual point of view. My powers have long been busy in these directions, and some day I shall compass what is lacking, by my activity and meditations, harmonizing it inwardly with everything already mine. There are sciences which I have still to explore thoroughly, for my outlook on the world can never be complete without their knowledge. Many types of humanity are still strange to me; there are ages and peoples that I know no better than the average man does, my imagination has not in its own way entered into their thought and character, they occupy no definite place in my picture of mankind's development. Many activities which have no place in my own being I do not understand, and I am frequently at a loss how to estimate their relation to all that is great and fine in humanity. I shall acquire all these things gradually, one with the other; the fairest prospect opens out before me. What a galaxy of individuals I see close at hand, men so different from myself yet all of them engaged in perfecting the humanity that is in them! What an amazing number of learned men are about me, who out of pride or hospitality offer me the golden fruit of their lives in handsome jars, and the plants of distant times and places too, transplanted to the fatherland by their faithful toil! Can fate enchain me so that I shall not be able to approach this goal of mine? Can it deny me the means of self-development, put me out of easy touch with the labors of the present generation and with the monuments of the past? Can it cast me out of this fair world in which I live into those barren wastes where contact with the rest of humanity is impossible, where vulgarity surrounds me on all sides with its everlasting monotony, and nothing lovely, nothing distinct stands out in the thick and sodden atmosphere? To be sure, this has befallen many, yet it can not happen to me; I defy that to which thousands have succumbed. A man must sell himself in order to become a slave, and fate dares bid only for one who offers himself at a price. What is it that lures the vacillating person away from the place where his spirit prospers? What can possibly impel him to throw away the finest treasures in cowardly folly, as the fleeing warrior does his weapons? It is the craving for base, external gain, it is the excitement of sensual desires already jaded so that the familiar draughts no longer satisfy. How could this happen to me in view of my despising such shadows! I have gained the position I occupy by industry and toil, with deliberate effort I have built a world of my own in which my spirit can flourish. How are firm connections like these to be loosened by some transient incitement whether of fear or of hope? How is some vain bagatelle to lure me from my true home and from the circle of my beloved friends?

But to continue living in this happy sphere and to become ever more closely related to it is not my only requirement; I long for another world. I still have many new ties to form; my heart must beat to the law of new loves as yet unknown to me, that the relation of these to the rest of my being may be revealed. I have experienced every kind of friendship, I have tasted the sweet joy of love with pure lips, I know what befits me in both relationships, what rule of life is appropriate to my nature. But the most sacred of all ties has to lift my life to a new level; some beloved soul and I must melt into one being, so that my humanity may touch other humanity in the finest of all relationships, and I may know the transfigured, higher life which will develop at this rebirth of freedom in me, the beginning of a new world for my regenerated self. I must be consecrated to paternal rights and duties, so that the maximum of power which freedom exercises over other free beings may not remain dormant in me, that I may show how he who believes in freedom preserves and protects reason in the young, and how in this great problem a discerning spirit can untangle the finest maze of his and other's rights. But will not fate overreach me just in respect to this dearest wish of my heart? Will not the world at this point take revenge upon my defiant freedom, upon my arrogant disrespect for its power? Where may she dwell with whom I might suitably link my life? Who can tell me whither I must go to seek her? For such a boon no sacrifice is too dear, no effort too great! But what if I should find her already tied, so that she hesitates to come to me? Shall I be able to liberate her? And if I do win her, can my will decide whether as husband I shall also enjoy fatherhood? Here I stand at the boundary where my will is limited by another freedom, and by the course of life, a mystery of nature. I have hope; man can do much; by strength of will and serious effort he surmounts many difficulties. But should hope and effort both prove vain, if all is denied me, am I then conquered at this point by my fate? Has it then really prevented my inner life from reaching a higher level, and succeeded by its caprice in limiting my development? The impossibility of outward accomplishment does not prevent an inner process; I should pity the world more than myself and my beloved, for having lost a beautiful and rare example, a phantom that has strayed from a more perfect future into the present, capable of giving warmth and life to the world's dead conceptions. As long as we belong to one another, she and I, imagination will transport us, though we have not actually met, into our lovely paradise. Not in vain have I seen the soul of woman in so many different forms, and come to know the characteristic charms of her sequestered life. The further I still was from marriage, the greater was my care to learn the nature of its sacred domain; I know what is right there, and is not. I have pictured to myself all its possible forms in their perfection, even as a distant, future freedom will reveal them, and I know exactly which of these forms is appropriate to me. It is thus that I also know her, the unknown love, with whom I could unite myself for life most intimately, and I am already attuned to the lovely life which we should lead together. Being obliged in my present unhappy solitude to undertake and arrange many things alone, to suppress much, and to practice much renunciation and control, in matters both great and small, there constantly hovers before me a vivid realization of how in that life all this would be different and much better. She too must surely find it so, wherever she may be, she who is so constituted that she could love me and find her satisfaction in me. The identical longing, something far more than an indefinite desire, lifts her, as it does me, above the barren actualities for which she was not intended, and if we should suddenly be brought together by a stroke of magic, nothing would be strange to us; we should walk easily and gracefully into our new life as if we had been engaged through fond acquaintance of long standing. And thus, even without that stroke of magic, we are not deprived inwardly of our higher life together. It is for this life and by it that we are fashioned, and only its external manifestation is lost to the world.

Oh, that men knew how to use this divine power of the imagination, which alone can free the spirit and place it far beyond coercion and limitation of any kind, and without which man's sphere is so narrow and precarious! How much actually touches each of us in the course of his brief life? How many sides of our nature would remain unformed and undeveloped, if man's inner life were limited to those few things with which he came into actual external contact? Yet men are such creatures of the senses in respect to morality that they do not even trust themselves unless some overt act testifies to the truth of their feelings. He who puts such limitations on himself must live to no purpose in the great society of mankind! The opportunity to behold its life and action can be of no avail to him; helplessly he must complain of the world's dull monotony and the languor of its movements. He is ever wishing for new conditions, for other external provocatives to action, and looking for new friends as soon as the old have made what possible impression they could upon his soul. Life is everywhere too slow for him. But suppose it did lead him into a thousand new paths at a quicker pace, could the infinite be thus exhausted in the brief span of an individual life? What men of this type cannot even wish for, I actually achieve through the inner play of my imagination. For me imagination supplies what reality withholds; by virtue of it I can put myself in the position of any other person I notice; my spirit bestirs itself, transforms the situation to accord with its nature, and judges in imagination just how it would act in such a case. To be sure, men's average judgments of other people's natures and actions are unreliable, for they reckon by some artificial rote or useless stereotype; and afterwards they act far otherwise than their previous judgments would lead them to do. But when the exercise of imagination is not merely mechanical, but accompanied by inner reflection, as it must be wherever there is true life, and when judgment is the conscious issue of such reflection, then the subject contemplated, though it be foreign to one's experience and only imagined, shapes the spirit, as much as if possessed by it in reality and dealt with externally. Thus in the future as in the past I shall take possession of the whole world by virtue of inner activity, and I shall make better use of things in quiet contemplation than if I had to respond to every quickly passing impression with an overt act. Every relationship makes a deeper impression in this way, the spirit grasps it more definitely, and one's own nature is more perfectly reproduced in free, unbiased judgments. What the external life really contributes in addition is thus only a confirmation and test of an inner life which is prior and richer; the development of the spirit is not confined within the narrow limits of the external. Hence I no longer complain when my lot in the world is monotonous, nor when its course is hectic and irrational. I know that my external life will never manifest or perfect all sides of my inner nature. It will never place me in circumstances of such magnitude that my action will decide the weal and woe of thousands, circumstances in which I could give outward proof that in comparison with one of reason's sublime and holy ideals all else is nought to me. Perhaps I shall never come into open conflict with the world and be able to show how little all that the world has power to give or to withhold can disturb my inner peace and integrity. But I myself know how I should act even in such circumstances, and I know that my spirit has long since been ready and prepared for everything of that kind. Thus, though I remain in seclusion, I nevertheless live upon the great and open stage of the world's actions. Thus, even in my solitude, I have already tied the knot with my beloved; our union is a fact, and indeed is the better part of my life. Thus, too, I shall surely keep possession of my only riches, the love of my friends, whatever may happen to them or to me in the future.

Men are indeed fearful that friendship will not last long, the mind seems to them fickle; a friend may change, his wonted love disappearing with his wonted disposition; loyalty is a rare treasure. And men are right. For if any of them look beyond utility in their friendships, it is the mere atmosphere surrounding a personality that they are prone to love, or perhaps some particular virtue, which they never trace to its inner root in the character, and if in the course of life's entanglements they come to miss these qualities, they are not ashamed to confess even after many years that they were mistaken in their friends. I am not favored with a fine figure or with anything else that is wont to catch the hearts of people at first sight, and yet everyone who has not seen into my inner nature creates for himself some superficial impression of me. Thus I come to be loved for a goodness of heart that I should not want to have, or for a modest nature which I have not got or for cleverness such as I heartily despise. This kind of love, to be sure, has often enough deserted me, and it does not belong among those riches that I prize. I consider that love alone a true possession, which my very self-evokes and wins over to me anew, time and again. How could I count as my own, an affection that is called forth entirely by an impression of me due to weak discernment. I wash myself clean of any such claim, in order not to deceive these people; but verily their false love shall not pursue me either, any longer than I can endure it. To throw them off will cost me but a single exhibition of my inner nature, one which they cannot mistake; I need but lead them straight to that which my own spirit treasures as its best, but which they cannot endure. Thus I shall rid me of this plague, that they who ought to hate me, love me and consider me one of their number. I shall gladly return to them the independence which they sacrificed to a false impression. But I can always count on those who are really devoted to me, who love my inner character; my spirit holds them fast and will never forsake them. They have known me, they have looked on my soul, and if they love my spirit as it is, they must love it ever more deeply, the more it develops and unfolds.

I am as certain of keeping this treasure as I am of my own being; I have never lost a friend who has been truly dear to me. You, who in the fresh bloom of youth, in the midst of a life that was strong and joyous, had to depart from our circle—yes, I can address the dear image that dwells in my bosom, and that continues to live on in my life, in my love and in my sorrow—never has my heart forsaken you. In my thought I have imagined your development, even as it would have taken place, had you lived to see the flames that now enkindle the world; your thinking has merged with mine, our love's conversation and the mutual contemplation of each other's souls never ceases, but continues to affect me as if you were living beside me as you formerly did. And you, my dear friends, who are still living in fact, though far from me, and who often send fresh impressions of your lives and thoughts, what matters distance to us? We were together a long while and were less close to one another than we are now; for what is being together, save community of spirit? What I do not see of your lives I construct for myself; you are present to me in all things, both inward and outward, that would vitally stir your souls, and a few words between us serve to confirm my imagination or to put it on the right track where I was in chance of error. You, who are even now with me in loving comradeship, you know how little I desire to roam abroad; I will stay in my place, and will not forego the fair opportunity: of exchanging life and thought with you at every moment. Where such communion is possible, there is my paradise. If you are possessed of a different thought, well and good: distance cannot separate us—But can death? Ah, what is death, but a greater distance?

Somber thought, that implacably shadows all meditation upon life and the future! I can assert that death will never part my friends from me, for I take up their lives in mine, and their influence upon me never ceases. But it is I myself who slowly perish in their death. The life of friendship is a sequence of harmonizing chords, to a keynote which dies out when the friend passes away. Of course, within oneself reechoing tones are heard without cease for a long while and the music is carried on; but the accompanying harmony in him, of which I was the keynote, has died away, and it was this that gave me my key, just as I gave him his. What I produced in him is no more, and thereby a part of my life is lost. Every creature that loves another kills something in that other through its death, and he who loses many of his friends is finally slain himself at their hands, since cut off from influencing those who were his world, his spirit is driven inward and forced to consume itself. There are two cases in which man's end is inevitable. He must perish for whom the death of friends has irretrievably destroyed the balance between the inner and the outer life. And he too must perish for whom this balance is otherwise destroyed, he who has attained the perfection of his individuality, and in whom, therefore, no further activity is essential, even though he be surrounded by the richest of worlds. A completely perfected being is a god, it could not endure the burden of life,1 and has no place in the world of mankind. Death, therefore, is a necessity, and may it be the mission of my freedom to bring me nearer to this necessity. May it be my highest goal to be able to wish to die! I wish to give myself to my friends so completely, and embrace their whole being so closely, that each may help to slay me with sweet pangs, when he leaves me, and I wish to perfect myself more and more, so that my soul may in this way also approach ever nearer the wish to die. The death of man is always the result of these two elements combined; not all my friends will leave me ere I die, nor shall I ever actually reach my goal of perfection. I shall approach my end from all sides in just proportion as befits the equipoise of my nature; of this good fortune I am assured by my perfect tranquility and my quiet contemplative life. For a nature such as mine the highest point is reached when its inner development seeks an external embodiment, since every kind of nature in its perfection approaches its opposite. The idea of perpetuating my inner being, and with it the whole outlook which humanity gave me, in a work of art is for me a premonition of death. As I first became aware of my maturity, this idea was born in me; now it waxes daily and assumes a definite form. Prematurely, I know, and yet voluntarily I shall release it from my mind, before the fire of life has died in me. For should I allow the work to ripen and grow perfect within me, my very being itself would pass away as soon as its faithful copy was ready for the world. It would have achieved its end.

Youth and Age

As the stroke of the clock tolls the hours, and the sun's course measures out the years, my life, as I am well aware, draws ever nearer the hour of death. But does it also approach old age, weak and broken old age, of which everyone bitterly complains, when without warning the zest of joyous youth has slipped away, and all health of spirit, all exuberance is gone? Why do men permit life's golden years to pass, and sighing bend their necks beneath a self-imposed yoke? There was a time when I myself believed the privileges of youth did not befit manhood; I thought to conduct myself quietly and prudently, preparing for years more drab by a wise resolve of renunciation. My spirit however, would not content itself within such narrow bounds, and I soon repented this life of bare economy. At the very first summons joyous youth returned, and ever since has held me in its protecting embrace. Were I now convinced that youth would escape me with the flight of years, I should voluntarily hasten to meet an early death, lest fear of certain misery to come embitter every good of the present, and incapacitate my life until finally I deserved an even worse end.

But I know that this cannot be true, because it should not be. Shall the free and immeasurable life of the spirit be spent before the life of the flesh is ended, which contains the seeds of death in its very first pulsations? Shall not my imagination always contemplate beauty with its full and wonted strength? Can I not always count on buoyancy of Spirit, responsiveness to good, and warmth of heart? Am I to listen with dread to the waves of time, and see them grind and channel me until I give way? Tell me, O heart, how many times the time just now spent upon this wretched thought may I still expect

177

to live before these horrors come to pass? Could I count them, I should think a thousand times as brief as one. But be not a fool, to prophecy the spirit's strength in terms of time, for time can never be its measure! The stars in their courses do not traverse equal distances in equal times; you must seek a higher calculus to comprehend their motion. And should the spirit follow meaner laws than they? No, nor does it do so. Old age, soured, bare, and hopeless, fetches many prematurely, and some evil spirit breaks off the bud of their youth before it has scarcely blossomed; others keep their vigor long; though white, their heads are unbowed, a fire still animates their eyes, and happy laughter graces their lips. Why should I not successfully fight off the death that lurks in hiding for me, even longer than he who has maintained his prime the longest? Ignoring the toll of years and the body's decay, why should I not by sheer force of will cling to youth's dear divinity until my last breath is drawn? For what is to explain this difference in aging, if not force of will? Is the spirit forsooth of a finite size and measure, which can be spent and exhausted? Is its strength used up by action and dissipated in every movement? Is it only misers who have been chary of their deeds that enjoy long life? If it be so, let shame and scorn smite all whose old age wears a fresh and happy look; for he deserves scorn who has been miserly with his youth.

Were time actually the measure of man's life and destiny, I should rather realize all my spiritual possibilities in a brief span; I should want to live a short life that I might keep young and vital while it lasted! What good are rays of light thinly diffused over a wide surface? There can be no revelation of power in them, no effective accomplishment. Of what avail is it to economize and conserve action, if you must weaken its inner content, and if finally you have nothing left anyway? Rather spend your life in a few years with brilliant prodigality, so that you may enjoy the sense of your strength, and be able to survey what you have amounted to. But man's measure and his destiny are not temporal; the spirit will not submit to such empirical delimitation. For what is there to break its power? What can it lose of its being by activity and by pouring itself out to others? What is there to consume it? I feel myself enriched and clarified by every action, stronger, and more sound; for in every act I receive some nourishment from humanity's common store, and in the process of growth my nature assumes a more definite character. Is this true only because I am still climbing up the hill of life? Perhaps, but when will this happy condition suddenly be reversed? When shall I begin to decline instead of growing by activity? And how will this great transformation be announced? If it comes, I can not help but recognize it, and if I recognize it, I shall rather choose to die, than to live in protracted misery, beholding in myself the impotence of human existence.

The decline of vigor and of strength is an ill that man inflicts upon himself; old age is but an idle prejudice, an ugly fruit of the mad delusion that the spirit is dependent on the body! But I know this madness, and its evil fruit shall not succeed in poisoning my healthy life. Does the spirit inhabit the fibers of my flesh, or are the two identical, that it needs must stiffen like a mummy when they are petrified? Let the body have its due. If the senses grow dull, and our impressions of reality's earthly images grow faint, then surely memory too will be dimmed, and many pleasures and delights will fade. But is this the life of the spirit? Is this the everlasting youth that I worship? If such things had power to weaken the spirit, how long had I already been old age's slave! How long ago should I have bade my youth a last farewell! But nothing that has hitherto been unable to disturb my energetic life, shall ever succeed in doing so. Am I not surrounded by others who have sharper senses and stronger bodies? Will they not always be about me as they are now to offer the service of their love? To lament my physical decline is of all things furthest from my mind! Why should that trouble me? Would it be such a misfortune, if I did forget the events of yesterday? Are the day's minutia the world in which I live? Is the sphere of my inner life limited to the impressions I get of those particular things that happen to exist within the narrow confines of my immediate physical environment? Whoever has loved youth only because it excelled in these immediate physical advantages, and whose inferior perception cannot grasp a higher calling, may justly complain of old age and its misery. But who will dare maintain that the presence of those great and sublime thoughts which the spirit produces out of its own depths is dependent on the body, and that a sense for true reality hinges on the functioning of one's frame? In order to contemplate humanity do I need this eye, the nerve of which already begins to weaken when my life is but half over? Or must my blood, which even now begins to flow slowly, rush more impetuously through my narrow veins, if I am to love all who deserve my love? Does the power of my will depend on the strength of my muscles, or on the marrow of my bones? Does courage depend upon my feeling in good health? Those who are thus physically favored are often enough deceived; death lurks in hidden corners, and suddenly springs upon them with sardonic laughter. What harm, then, if I already know, where my own death lies waiting? But perhaps repeated pain, or manifold sufferings, can so depress the spirit as to incapacitate it for its own unique and proper functions? Why! to resist such pains is also a function of the spirit; they too call forth sublime thoughts for their relief. And the spirit can find no evil in anything that merely changes its activity from one form to another.

Yes, in my advanced years I shall still have the same strength of spirit, and I shall never lose my keen zest for life. That which now rejoices me, shall ever give me joy; my will shall remain strong, and my imagination active, and nothing shall wrest from me the magic key which opens the mysterious portals of the higher world; nor shall love's ardent flame ever be quenched. I will not see the dread infirmities of old age; I vow a mighty scorn of all adversity that does not touch the aim of my existence, and I pledge myself to an eternal Youth.

But am I not repudiating good along with evil? Is old age sheer weakness when compared with youth? Why then is it that mankind honors a grey head, even though it shows no trace of this eternal youth, freedom's finest fruit? Alas, often it is only because some people lead their lives in an atmosphere like that of a cellar, which will for a long time preserve a corpse from decay, and such men are popularly venerated as sacred bodies. People think of the soul as like a grapevine; be it even of poor quality, it improves and is more highly prized when it grows old. Nay more! they talk much of virtues peculiar to life's riper years, of sober wisdom, cool self-possession, a rich experience, a poised and unassailable perfection in one's understanding of this variegated world. Youth's charm, they say, is only the evanescent blossom of human nature, but the mature fruit is old age and what it brings the soul. Then only are the innermost depths of human nature ripe for enjoyment when they have been completely purified by air and sun, and brought to some significant and beautiful perfection. O ye northern barbarians, who do not know the happier clime, where fruit and blossom burst forth together, and race side by side in all their glory to a joint fulfillment! Is the world so cold and unfriendly that the human spirit may not emulate this higher beauty and perfection? Of course, everyone cannot have all that is good and beautiful, but diverse gifts are given to diverse persons and not apportioned to the different seasons of life. Each man is a plant of unique growth, but he can continually bear fruit and flower at the same time according to his kind. Whatever can be harmoniously realized in a single individual, he can cultivate simultaneously and possess permanently; he not only can but should.

How does man acquire discreet wisdom and ripe experience? Are they granted him from on high. and is it foreordained that he shall not receive them until he can prove that youth is passed? I am conscious of acquiring them at this very moment; it is precisely the urge of youth and the quickened life of the spirit that brings them forth. To inspect all things, to absorb them in the innermost sense, to master the force of random emotions lest tears either of joy or grief dim the spirit's vision or cloud its impressions, to proceed readily from one thing to another, and being of insatiable energy to assimilate even the experience of others by rehearsing their deeds in imagination, such is the active life of youth, and such too is the process by which wisdom and experience come into being. The livelier the imagination, the more active the spirit, the more is their growth hastened and prospered. And when they have been acquired, is the vigorous life that produced them no longer appropriate? Are then these supreme virtues ever perfected? If they were born in youth and by reason of youth, will they not always require the same energy to maintain and further their growth? Mankind, however, is deceived by a hypocritical vanity in respect to this its greatest blessing, and its hypocrisy is rooted in depths of narrowest ignorance. Youth's restlessness is supposed to imply the urge of a seeker, and seeking is not thought becoming to one who has reached the end of life; such a one should clothe himself in the repose of idleness that respected symbol of life's fulfillment, and in emptiness of desire, the sign of complete understanding. Such should be the deportment of old age, they say, lest seeming still to be a seeker, man descend into the grave amid laughter mocking his vain efforts. But only those who have sought what is cheap and vulgar may pride themselves on having found all they desire! What I aspire to know and make my own is infinite, and only in an infinite series of attempts can I completely fashion my own being. The spirit that drives man forward, and the constant appeal of new goals, that can never be satisfied by past achievements, shall never depart from me. It is man's peculiar pride, to know that his goal is infinite, and yet never to halt on his way, to know that at some point on his journey he will be engulfed, and yet when he sees that point, to make no change either in himself or in his circumstances, nor in any wise to slacken his pace. Hence it is fitting that he should ever pursue his way in the carefree buoyancy of youth. I shall never consider myself old until I am perfect, and I shall never be perfect, because I know and desire what I should. Furthermore, the excellences of old age cannot conflict with those of youth, for not only do the qualities esteemed in old age develop in youth, but old age in its turn nourishes the young and tender life. It is generally conceded that youth fares better when ripe old age takes an interest in it, and in the same way a man's own inner youth is enhanced, if he acquires in early life the spiritual qualities of maturity. A practiced eye surveys its field more quickly, and a person of experience grasps a situation more readily, and that love which springs from a higher level of self-development must needs be more intense. Wherefore I shall preserve my youthful vigor and I shall enjoy its zest unto the last. Unto the last I shall gain in strength and in vitality with every act, and with each step in my self-development I shall become more capable of love. I shall marry my youth to my old age, that the latter too may enjoy exuberance and be permeated with vivifying warmth. For what is it, after all, of which men complain in old age? not of consequences that necessarily follow from experience, wisdom, and self-development. Does a treasury of accumulated ideas make a man less sensitive, so that nothing either old or new interests him? Do established words of wisdom at last give way to disquieting doubts that vitiate all action? Is self-development a consuming fire that leaves the soul an inert mass? The general complaint is only that youth has fled. And why does youth fail man? Because in his youth he has lacked maturity. Let there be a double marriage. Let the strength of years enter into your robust spirit at once to preserve its youth, that in later years youth may protect you against the weakness of old age. The usual division of life into youth and age ought never to be made. He debases himself who wishes first to be young, and then old, who allows himself to be controlled first by what is called the spirit of youth, and only afterwards wishes to follow what is considered the counsel of maturity. Life cannot bear this separation of its elements. There is a two-fold activity of the spirit that should exist in its entirety at every time of life, and it is the perfection of human development ever to become more intimately and more clearly conscious of both its aspects, assigning to each its own peculiar and proper function.

The individual existence of a plant is perfected in its blossom, but the world attaches supreme value to its fruit, which serves as protection to the seed of future generations, and is a gift which every creature must offer in order that the rest of nature may receive his life. So too, the supreme thing for a human being is the spirited life of youth, and woe to him whom it forsakes, but the world desires him to grow old, that his life may bear fruit, the sooner the better. Wherefore set your life in accord with this fact once and for all. It is a lesson which old age teaches men all too late, when time has dragged them thither in its chains, but by a firm resolution of your free will you may at once make it your rule in all matters upon which the world has a claim. Wherever fruit appears as the spontaneous result of your life's free flowering, let it develop to the world's advantage, and may there be hidden in it a fertile seed destined to unfold one day into a new life of its own. But let whatever you offer to the world be fruit. Do not sacrifice the least part of your being itself in mistaken generosity! Let no bud be broken off, nor the smallest leaf plucked, through which you receive nourishment from the surrounding world! On the other hand, do not put forth mere foliage unpruned and unpleasing, in which some poisonous insect may hide and sting you. If it is not part of your own proper development, or the growth of new members, let it be genuine fruit, engendered within the heart of the spirit, a free act testifying to its youthful creative energy. But when it is once conceived, such fruit should emerge from the province of the inner life; then let its further development conform to the laws of outward behavior. Then let shrewdness and sober wisdom and cool discretion take it in charge, that what your love generously intended for the world may actually prove to its benefit. Then weigh means and end with care, take heed and be circumspect with cautious misgiving, seek counsel of work and power, despise no pains, and wait for propitious moments with untiring patience.

Woe unto me, if my youth, with its vitality that brooks no restraint and its restless imagination, should ever meddle with the affairs of old age, and failing to succeed in the realm of action, which is not its proper province, should thereby waste the strength of its inner life! Only such as are ignorant of inner energies may perish thus, those who, misunderstanding the spiritual urge, wish to be young in their outward behavior. They expect fruit to ripen in a moment even as a blossom opens in a night; each of their projects crowds upon the heels of another, and none matures. Every enterprise, which they commence, is destroyed in the rapid alternation of their conflicting plans. And when they have thus wasted the loveliest half of life in vain attempts, doing and achieving nought, because to do and to accomplish was their only aim, then they condemn the free imagination and the youthful life. Nought but old age is left them, weak and miserable as it must be, wherever youth has been used up and driven out. Lest it flee from me also, I shall not abuse it; I shall not expect its service in matters that are not its proper sphere; I shall keep it within the limits of its own domain, that it may meet with no injury. But there in truth it shall have full sway, now and forever in unmolested freedom, nor shall any law, the proper sphere of which is to govern external actions, cramp my inner life.

May my inner activity and all that affects it, in so far as the world has no claim upon it and it concerns only my own growth, bear youth's colors everlastingly, and may it proceed wholly from an inner impulse with a gracious and perfect joy. O my soul, let no rule be imposed on your coming in and going out, your hours of meditation and reflection! Heartily despise such alien legislation and banish the thought which would put the free movement of your life under the sign of a dead letter. Let no one persuade you that one thing must wait upon the completion of another! Proceed, if you like, with buoyant step; what you have done lives on in you, and you will find it again when you return. Do not anxiously ponder what to begin and what will come of it! You alone are in the making, and whatever you can will, is also part of you. Shun frugal behavior! Let life be unconfined: no power is ever lost, unless you repress it within yourself, and leave it unused. Let not your will for today be determined by your wish for tomorrow! Take shame, free spirit that you are, if ought within you should become subservient to the rest; no part of your being may be mere means to an end, for one is as precious as another. Wherefore whatever you become, let it be for its own sake. A stupid self-deception to think that you ought to want what you do not want! Let not the world tell you how you should serve it and when! Laugh to scorn its silly pretensions, spirited youth, and do not brook restraint. Whatever you give is a gift of your freedom, for the resolve to benefit the world must issue from within you. Attempt nothing unless it proceeds freely from a love and desire within your soul. And let no limit be set upon your love, no measure whether of kind or of duration! If it is your own, who can demand it of you? Is not its law entirely within you? Then who may command it in any respect? Be ashamed to depend on other's opinions in such matters of holiest import. Blush for that false shame which fears lest people may not understand you when you reply to the questioner: "Such is the reason of my love." Let not yourself be troubled in the fullness and joy of your inner life by anything external whatsoever! Who would choose to combine within himself elements that are incompatible, and thus be soured in his soul? Grieve not for what you cannot be or do! Who would be ever gazing toward the impossible in empty aspiration and turning covetous eyes upon goods that are not his?

Thus is my inner life joyous and untrammeled! And how should time and destiny ever teach me another philosophy? I give the world its due; in my outward behavior I strive for order and wisdom, discretion and proportion. Indeed, what reason have I to disdain anything that proceeds so readily and freely and happily from my inner being and its activity? By observing the world one will gain all this in rich measure without effort. But in beholding himself, man triumphs over discouragement and weakness, for from the consciousness of inner freedom there blossoms eternal youth and joy. On these have I laid hold, nor shall I ever give them up, and so I can see with a smile my eyes growing dim, and my blond locks turning white. Nought can happen to affright my heart, and the pulse of my inner life will beat with vigor until death.

END NOTES

EPIGRAPH

1. Opening paragraph of *The Monologen*

PREFACE

1. Karl Barth, *The Theology of Schleiermacher: Lectures at Gottingen*, Winter Semester of 1923/24, Dietrich Ritschl ed. (Eugene, Or: Wipf & Stock, 1982), xiii. It should be noted that here that Barth was very critical of Schleiermacher's theology, on the whole, and this quote was meant as more of a commentary of his influence and less as a compliment. This will be discussed further in my critical introduction below.

2. The dialectical theology movement, led by Karl Barth in the 1920s, was a directed response to liberal theology, of which Schleiermacher was considered an exemplification.

3. Friedrich Schleiermacher, *On Religion: Speeches to its Cultured Despisers*, John Oman, trans. (New York: Harper Brothers, 1958), 15.

4. See *Introduction to the Monologen: Father of Modern Theology* below, for a more detailed discussion.

5. Friedrich Schleiermacher, *The Christian Faith*, trans. H.R. Mackintosh (London: T&T Clark, 1999), 12

6. See *Introduction to the Monologen: Father of Modern Theology* below, for a more detailed discussion.

7. Friedrich Schleiermacher, *Hermeneutics and Criticism*, Andrew Bowie ed. (Cambridge: Cambridge University Press, 1998), 23.

8. See Friedrich Schleiermacher, *Introduction to Christian Ethics*, John C. Shelley trans. (Nashville: Abington Press, 1989), 36.

9. Ibid, 38.

10. See Friedrich Schleiermacher, *The Life of Jesus* (Philadelphia: Fortress Press, 1975) and Friedrich Schleiermacher, *Luke: A Critical Study* (Lewiston, New York: Edwin Mellen Press, 1993).

FATHER OF MODERN THEOLOGY

1. Immanuel Kant, "*What is Enlightenment?*", in Foundations of the Metaphysics of Morals and What is Enlightenment, tr. by L. W. Beck, (New York: Liberal Arts Press, 1959).

2. Immanuel Kant, *Religion within the Boundaries of Mere Reason,* trans. Werner S. Pluhar (Indianapolis, IN: Hackett Publishing Company), 1.

3. Brian Duignan, *The Categorical Imperative,* Encyclopedia Britannica online. Last modified 11/23/2023. https://www.britannica.com/topic/categorical-imperative.

4. Immanuel Kant, Religion and Rational Theology, ed. And trans. Allen W. Wood and George di Giovanni (Cambridge: Cambridge University Press, 1996), 190.

5. Ibid.

6. Immanuel Kant, *Critique of Practical Reason*, trans. Lewis White Beck (Indianapolis, IN: bobs-Merrill, 1959), 130.

7. Ibid 118.

8. David Hume, Dialogues Concerning Natural Religion, ed. Richard Popkin (Hackett Publishing Company: Cambridge, 1980), 31.

9. Michael K. Kellogg, The Wisdom of the Enlightenment (Prometheus Books: Lanham, Maryland, 2022), 219.

10. David Hume, *An Inquiry Concerning Human Understanding*, ed. Charles W. Hendel (Indianapolis, IN: Bobbs-Merrill, 1955), 122.

11. Ibid., 123.

12. Dennis G. Rasmussen, *The Infidel and the Professor*, (Princeton, NJ: Princeton University Press, 2017) 248.

13. Stephen D. Morrison, *Schleiermacher in Plain English*, (Columbus, Ohio: Beloved Press, 2019), xvi-xvii.

14. Ibid., xvii.

15. It should be noted that Kant likely was responsive to Kant because he felt he had to be. From the standpoint of indebtedness to an underlying philosophic motif, Schleiermacher owed that to Plato. See Julia A. Lamm, *Schleiermacher's Plato* (Berlin: De Gruyter, 2023).

16. Friedrich Schleiermacher, *The Monologen*, Horace Leland Friess trans. (Eugene, OR: Wipf and Stock Publishers, 2002), xxvii.

17. Ibid., xxiv.

18. Ibid., xxxix.

19. Schleiermacher would always consider himself a Moravian. But now he dubbed himself, "A Moravian of a higher order." Quoted from Ian S. Wishart, *Schleiermacher's Interpretation of the Bible* (Eugene, OR: Wipf and Stock Publishing), 9

20. Friedrich Schleiermacher, *The Christian Faith*, trans. H.R. Mackintosh (London: T&T Clark), 5.

21. Ibid., 16.

22. Friedrich Schleiermacher, *On Religion: Speeches to its Cultured Despisers*, trans. John Ohman (New York: Harper and Brothers Publishing, 1958), 87.

23. Julia A. Lamm, *The Early Philosophical Roots of Schleiermacher's Notion of Gefühl, 1788-1794*, Harvard Theological Review, 87 (1994): 71.

24. Ibid., 72.

25. Ibid., 73.

26. Ibid., 84.

27. Friedrich Schleiermacher, On Religion: Speeches to its Cultured Despisers, trans. John Ohman (New York: Harper and Brothers Publishing, 1958), 20, 25-26.

28. Ibid., 28.

29. Friedrich Schleiermacher, *The Christian Faith*, trans. H.R. Mackintosh (London: T&T Clark), 133-134.

30. Ibid., 12.

31. Ludwig Feuerbach, The Essence of Christianity trans. George Elliot (New York: Harper and Row, 1957) 9-10.

32. Quote from James Duke, *On the Glaubenslehre: Translator's Introduction* (Ann Arbor: Scholars Press, 1981), 15.

33. See Thandeka, *The Embodied Self: Friedrich Schleiermacher's Solution to Kant's Problem of the Empirical Self* (Albany: State of New York Press, 1995), 1,4. See also Gordon E. Michalson, Jr. *Fallen Freedom: Kant on Radical Evil and Moral Regeneration* (Cambridge: Cambridge University Press, 1990) 78-79.

34. Thandeka, 18.

35. Friedrich Schleiermacher, *Dialektik, aus Schleiermachers Handschriftlichem Nachlasse*, ed. Ludwig Jonas (Berlin: Georg Reimer, 1839) 429.

36. Ibid., 532.

37. Thandeka, 85.

38. *Dialektik*, 414.

39. Thandeka, 92.

40. William James, *The Varieties of Religious Experience: A Study of Human Nature* (New York: Penguin Books, 1982), pp. 387-388.

41. Thandeka, 94. As Thandeka summarizes, "*Gefühl* is the content of *Anschauung's* frame of mind." Thandeka, 96.

42. *On Religion*, 43-44.

43. See Friedrich Schleiermacher, *On the Glaubenslehre, trans. James Duke* (Ann Arbor: Scholars Press, 1981), 88-89. He states, "And so I want to say that I am a real supernaturalist...But I fail to see what is to be gained from all of this." By 'this," Schleiermacher was referencing the need to posit God acting outside of the realm of nature.

44. Ibid., 88.

45. *The Christian Faith*, 178.

46. Ibid., 179.

47. Ibid., 184.

48. Ibid., 403.

49. Ibid., 405.

50. Ibid., 405-406.

51. Friedrich Schleiermacher, Brief Outline of Theology as a Field of Study, 3rd ed, trans. Terrence Tice (Louisville: Westminster John Knox Press, 2011) 46.

52. *Christian Faith*, 608.

53. See Schleiermacher's discussion of the subject in *On the Glaubenshlehre*, 55-58. Here he addresses the concern that he diminished the importance of the doctrine of the Trinity by relegating it to the ending of *The Christian Faith*.

54. *Christian Faith*, 385.

55. Dole, Andrew. "Schleiermacher and Religious Naturalism" In *Schleiermacher, the Study of Religion, and the Future of Theology: A Transatlantic Dialogue* edited by Brent W. Sockness and Wilhelm Gräb, 15-26. Berlin, New York: De Gruyter, 2010. https://doi.org/10.1515/9783110 216349.2.15.

56. Ibid., 15.

57. See "Millenarianism." Merriam-Webster.com Dictionary, Merriam-Webster, https://www.merr iam-webster.com/dictionary/millenarianism. Accessed 26 Dec. 2023. Millenarians were a radical sect who believed in an imminent coming millennium and the bringing about of an idealistic society by radical action.

58. *The Monologen*, xiv.

59. Ibid., xv.

60. *The Christian Faith*, 546.

61. *Schleiermacher in Plain English*, 4.

62. *The Christian Faith*, 139.

63. For a more extensive discussion on this matter, see Morrison's *Schleiermacher in Plain English* pp. 3-16.

64. *The Christian Faith*, 547

65. Ibid., 549.

66. We are fortunate to have preserved many of Schleiermacher's sermons preached during his tenure at Trinity Church in Berlin. See Friedrich Schleiermacher, *Christmas Sermons: Displays in a Theology of Christian Faith and Life (1790-1833)*, Terrence Tice, ed. (Eugene: Cascade Books), 2019.

67. Friedrich Schleiermacher, *Introduction to Christian Ethics*, John C. Shelley, trans. (Nashville: Abington Press, 1989), 95.

68. Schleiermacher has not only received the title of Father on Modern Theology, but his work in translation has also earned him the additional title Father of Hermeneutics. See Friedrich Schleiermacher, *Hermeneutics and Criticism and Other Writings*, Andrew Bowie, ed. (Cambridge: Cambridge University Press, 1995)

69. Terrence Tice, *Schleiermacher* (Nashville: Abington Press, 2005), 14.

70. Friedrich Schleiermacher, *An Essay on the Trinity: On the Discrepancy between Sabellian and Athanasian Method of Representing the doctrine of the Trinity*, trans. M. Stuart (Columbus: Beloved Publishing, 2018), 60.

71. Karl Barth, The Theology of Schleiermacher: Lectures at Gottingen, Winter Semester of 1923/24, Dietrich Ritschl ed. (Eugene: Wipf & Stock, 1982), xiii.

72. *On Religion*, 1.

73. Ibid., 25, 41.

74. *Letters*, v. 1, pp. 227-228.

75. *The Monologen*, xi.

76. See page 127.

77. Ibid., 130.

78. Ibid., 132.

79. Ibid., 136.

80. Ibid., 137.

81. Ibid., 138.

82. Ibid., 139.

83. Ibid.

84. Ibid., 145.

85. Ibid., 151.

86. Ibid., 153.

87. Ibid., 155.

88. Ibid.

89. Ibid., 159.

90. Ibid., 165.

91. Ibid., 167.

92. Ibid., 170.

93. Ibid., 172.

94. Ibid., 176.

95. Ibid., 177.

96. Ibid., 178.

97. Ibid., 179.

98. Ibid., 185. This essay is an adaptation and expansion of a chapter in my forthcoming book, *Naturally God: The Case for Christian Naturalism.*

To contact Chad Bahl for speaking engagements,
please email cbahl2000@yahoo.com.

Many Voices. One Message.

quoir.com

Printed in Great Britain
by Amazon

45203829R00121